CAMBRIDGE MUSIC HANDBOOKS

Musorgsky: *Pictures at an Exhibition*

CAMBRIDGE MUSIC HANDBOOKS

GENERAL EDITOR Julian Rushton

Cambridge Music Handbooks provide accessible introductions to major musical works, written by the most informed commentators in the field.

With the concert-goer, performer and student in mind, the books present essential information on the historical and musical context, the composition, and the performance and reception history of each work, or group of works, as well as critical discussion of the music.

Other published titles

Musorgsky: *Pictures at an Exhibition*

Michael Russ

University of Ulster at Jordanstown

Published by the Press Syndicate of the University of Cambridge
The Pitt Building, Trumpington Street, Cambridge CB2 1RP
40 West 20th Street, New York, NY 10011–4211, USA
10 Stamford Road, Oakleigh, Victoria 3166, Australia

© Cambridge University Press 1992

First published 1992

A catalogue record for this book is available from the British Library

Library of Congress cataloguing in publication data
Russ, Michael.
Musorgsky: Pictures at an Exhibition / Michael Russ.
p. cm. – (Cambridge music handbooks)
Includes bibliographical references and index.
ISBN 0 521 38442 7 (hardback). – ISBN 0 521 38607 1 (paperback).
1. Mussorgsky, Modest Petrovich, 1839–1881. Kartinki s vystavki.
I. Title. II. Series.
ML410.M97R9 1992
786.2'1896–dc20 91–32687 CIP MN

ISBN 0 521 38442 7 hardback
ISBN 0 521 38607 1 paperback

Transferred to digital printing 1999

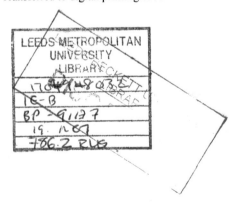
ALHP

Contents

Contents

Illustrations

Preface

In his study of Musorgsky written in the years coming up to the Second World War, M. D. Calvocoressi says of *Pictures at an Exhibition*: 'the whole suite ... is an attractive but not particularly significant work'. Such a remark might surprise us today when this piece is perhaps the most popular of Musorgsky's compositions. But there is sense in what Calvocoressi says; after all, is not this just a collection of ten rather brief and not terribly idiomatic piano pieces separated by little interludes? Similar collections of pieces by other composers are generally considered in a lesser light than their symphonic, chamber and operatic output; why should a book be devoted to Musorgsky's *Pictures*?

The answer lies both in the unique conception of the original work and its unparalleled history at the hands of editors and transcribers. Indeed, most of us first come to *Pictures* in Ravel's orchestration of Rimsky-Korsakov's version of Musorgsky's text. There is no other instrumental work like this one with its social messages from nineteenth-century Russia, its saturation in folk music and culture, and its innovative harmonic language all wrapped up in an alluringly colourful exterior. No other work has attracted so many orchestrators of such high calibre and yet left us with the feeling that the 'perfect' orchestration is beyond the grasp of any of them; no other nineteenth-century work raises so acutely the issue of authenticity and the question of what it is morally acceptable to do to another man's composition.

Musorgsky's *Pictures* warrant book-length treatment because of the myriad issues that surround them. To understand them fully we must know something about Musorgsky's artistic philosophy and matters such as Populism and realism and about the illustrations and their artist, Victor Hartman. One can enjoy Musorgsky's *Pictures* as pure music in Ravel's superbly crafted orchestration. But if ever there was a work where one benefits from knowledge of the stimuli that led to its creation and of the layers of meaning that the composer places on top of the original pictures it is this one. In a recent interview, Vladimir Ashkenazy, a pianist and conductor with a particular affinity for this work, who has produced his own orchestration, described the Russian mind as 'suspicious'; it never takes the obvious meaning, it always looks for something deeper. So it must be when we look at Musorgsky's *Pictures*. These little pieces do not simply turn Hartman's illustrations and designs into music, they bring them to life, creating little scenes out of them which, in turn, may carry messages about Russian culture and society.

Above all, this is Russian music. Although not all of the pictures are set in Russia, Musorgsky views them all from a Russian perspective, and the innovative qualities of the work have their roots in Russian soil. Partly for this reason, and also because for Musorgsky the communication of his message in a direct but artistic way is all important, we should not judge this piece by German standards of technical sophistication. The complex harmonic, contrapuntal and formal procedures of German music have no place here, since they might draw attention to themselves and detract from the matters under expression (something that Ravel's orchestration also does). Musorgsky's failure to use these techniques in a thoroughgoing, grammatically correct way has little to do with ignorance and poor training but everything to do with what he was trying to achieve.

Students of this work will have noticed that its Russian title 'Kartinki s vystavki' is either translated as 'Pictures *at* an Exhibition' or as 'Pictures *from* an Exhibition'. The latter title is a more exact translation of the Russian, but since the former is more often found we retain it here, usually abbreviated to *Pictures*.

In spelling the names of Russian musicians the transliterations are those in *The New Grove*. For the name Hartman the single 'n' at the end corresponds to the single character in the original cyrillic. Dates given in two forms recognise that the Russians continued to use the Julian calendar which, in the nineteenth century, lagged twelve days behind the Gregorian one used in the West. In quotations which give only one date it is the old system (O. S.). The full titles and various subtitles of each piece are given in Chapter 5. In the remainder of the book the obvious abbreviated forms are used. Bar numbers correspond to those in Schandert and Ashkenazy's Vienna Urtext Edition, which is the only edition I recommend (see Chapter 3; the next best edition is Hellmundt's Urtext, published by Peters, Leipzig). In discussing some of the orchestrations, cuts and alterations necessitate referring to rehearsal figures.

Acknowledgements

I would like to thank the following institutions and individuals who provided me with assistance and information: Robert Grossman (Philadelphia Orchestra Library), Dr Edwin E. Heilakka (Curator of the Leopold Stokowski Collection), Kauko Karalainen (Music Library, Finnish Radio), Lawrence Leonard, Evans Mirageas (Boston Symphony Orchestra) and Rosalind Woodall (Royal Academy of Music Library). Professor Marcus Wheeler (The Queen's University of Belfast) and Maria Marquise provided translations from Russian. The National Sound Archive, Stanford Archive of Recorded Sound and the publishers J. W. Chester, Boosey and Hawkes, Fazer Music Inc., International Music Company (Alfred A. Kalmus and Co.), Robert Lienau & Co. (Peters Edition) provided me with materials, as did Harrison Parrott Ltd. and the Decca Record Company Ltd. Professors Julian Rushton (University of Leeds) and Edward Garden (University of Sheffield) read and made invaluable suggestions on the manuscript; but the shortcomings remain those of the author. I also extend my gratitude to Penny Souster and the staff at Cambridge University Press, without whom the project would not have been possible.

Hartman's designs for 'Chicks' and 'The Great Gate at Kiev' are reproduced from copies kindly made available by the Institute of Russian Literature (Pushkin House) in St Petersburg. Translations of extracts from Musorgsky's letters and documents are reprinted by kind permission of publishers Da Capo Press and University Microfilms International.

My thanks too to the Humanities Faculty of the University of Ulster who made time and money available and to colleagues there who made many helpful suggestions and lent me materials.

1

'Pictures at an Exhibition' and nineteenth-century music

Modest Musorgsky (1839–81) composed *Pictures at an Exhibition* in 1874. Apart from the orchestral tone poem *St John's Night on the Bare Mountain*, it is his only substantial instrumental composition. Musorgsky's *Pictures* makes a unique contribution to the golden age of European piano music, an age brought about by steady advances in piano technology and the dissemination of virtuosi, instruments and teachers throughout Europe. During the first half of the nineteenth century many foreign pianists and teachers came to the cosmopolitan capital, St Petersburg, notably Clementi (who established a piano warehouse), Field and Henselt. But it was not until the dying years of the century that a Russian piano school of native composers and performers emerged. During the first three-quarters of the century only two very different masterworks, Balakirev's Lisztian *Islamey* and Musorgsky's in some ways unpianistic *Pictures* stand out.

Musorgsky, able to perform a concerto by Field at the age of nine, began piano lessons with his mother. On being sent to school in St Petersburg from 1849 to 1853 he took lessons with the best teacher in the city, the Pole Anton Herke. Herke, a pupil of Henselt, introduced Musorgsky to a wide range of European piano music and turned him into an excellent pianist.

After preparatory school Musorgsky entered the Guards' cadet school where debauchery rather than serious academic study was the order of the day and the seeds of the alcoholism that later killed him were sown. The scholarly Musorgsky was out of the ordinary, spending much time studying philosophy, history and foreign languages: the latter being reflected in the variety of languages employed in *Pictures*. Musorgsky entered the Preobrazhensky Guards in 1856 having already composed his *Porte-Enseigne Polka* and sketched an opera. That he knew little of musical theory was of small consequence since, for the handsome Guards' officer, pianism and an ability to compose trivial miniatures was all that was required for an entry into fashionable society.

Musorgsky lived nearly all his life in St Petersburg; despite the foreign

1

locations of several pieces in *Pictures* he never left his native land. Foreign composers, notably purveyors of Italian opera, dominated the 'serious' Russian musical scene in the city until the 1860s. There were orchestral and choral concerts of music by the German 'greats' but orchestral players were either from the theatre pits or amateurs and, for a time, concerts were only allowed during Lent when the Imperial theatres were closed. Opportunities for performing orchestral works by Russian composers were rare and it was in the opera house that they began to make their mark.

As a young Guards' officer, Musorgsky was fortunate in being introduced into the salon of Dargomïzhsky, and to Mili Balakirev (1837–1910). Musorgsky's senior by just two years, Balakirev had, through a rare capacity for self-education, managed to overcome the difficulties posed by the lack of formal musical training and from the age of twenty was advising aspiring Russian composers. He took Musorgsky under his wing playing duet arrangements of works by Beethoven, Schumann, Liszt, Glinka and others with him and discussing and analysing their structure. The Balakirev circle were intent on creating a new Russian music building on the innovations of Glinka, commonly regarded as the father of Russian music.

The dogmatic, obstinate Balakirev gave advice harshly and emphasised innovativeness, originality and the pragmatic acquisition of skills. His first reactions to Musorgsky were guarded and these early doubts persisted because the two men were on different artistic wavelengths. Musorgsky had little interest in, or talent for, extended instrumental composition. He was to find his true genius in realistic vocal works. His only major piano work was not to be a sonata, but the loosely arranged collection of descriptive pieces that form the subject of this book. Balakirev only encouraged Musorgsky to write instrumental, symphonic, sonata-form compositions. Musorgsky's Allegro in C for piano duet of 1858, his only piece in sonata form, is not a success. Of much more significance for Musorgsky was Balakirev's interest in folk music and his ability to use it to transform his own musical language in an innovative and original way. Certain harmonic influences of Balakirev can be identified in Musorgsky's weaker piano pieces, but *Pictures*, written when their paths had diverged, is largely free of Balakirevian fingerprints.

By 1862 Balakirev, Borodin, Cui, Musorgsky and Rimsky-Korsakov had been brought together as 'The Five', the Balakirev circle, or the 'Mighty Handful' as Vladimir Stasov (1824–1906) dubbed them. Balakirev became their leader and Stasov their artistic adviser. 'The Five' represent the difficulties faced by Russian composers particularly well. With the exception of Balakirev they were all aristocratic amateurs dabbling in composition, without professional training, something for which they were criticised by their contemporaries in the St Petersburg Conservatory.

Stasov prompted and guided Musorgsky throughout his life and is the dedicatee of *Pictures*. 'To you Généralissime, the sponsor of the Hartman Exhibition in remembrance of our dear Victor, June 27, 74' is written slantwise in the corner of the title page of Musorgsky's autograph. Stasov worked in the art department of the St Petersburg Public Library. His secure income and access to materials in this post put him in a position to influence profoundly the course of Russian music and art in the second half of the nineteenth century through criticism, writing, reviewing and personal contact. The title 'Généralissime' (he was also known as a 'pusher' (tolkatel) and a 'spurrer' (shpora))[1] reflects Stasov's influence and energetic character, ever pushing on the artists he adopted and providing them with ideas and materials. Stasov first met Musorgsky in 1857, but like Balakirev had thought little of him. Only in the 1870s did he come to realise that Musorgsky's work was the musical embodiment of the views he espoused. From this point on he typically, as with other artists who gained his support, became an almost overly enthusiastic supporter.

Stasov had travelled through Europe and knew the best and most progressive of its culture including the music of Schumann, Liszt, Berlioz and Wagner (Stasov and the rest of the Balakirev circle despised the latter). For him, native art had to develop not only by incorporating folk-inspired Russianness, but also by achieving the high artistic standards, and the sophistication and progressiveness of structure apparent in Western music. As a critic he sought to explain, educate and reveal meaning in the service of art for the people, art with a social conscience and message. Such is the intention of his remarks on *Pictures* discussed in later chapters.

Genre

Musorgsky's *Pictures* is a collection of short pieces, free from sonata form and demonstrating the power of folk music to transform rather than decorate the musical language. In a sense it brings on to a higher plane the mixture of tiny piano pieces he played with his mother and also in the salons of St Petersburg, and the folk music he heard in the countryside. His style is often rough-hewn and totally free from academicism, owing nothing to the purely musical sensitivity and elegance of composers like Field. His mode of expression is original, individual and direct; whatever the pianistic abilities of the composer, the medium is subservient to the message.

In his self-portrait Musorgsky records that as a 'relaxation' from his work on the operas *Khovanshchina* and *Sorochintsy Fair*, he composed an 'Album Series on the genius architect Hartman'.[2] An 'Album Series' is among the loosest of musical genres. The word 'album', as well as its appropriate association with the visual arts, implies randomness, slightness, even scrappiness, and a freedom to select what one wishes. This places *Pictures* among the many collections of piano miniatures assembled by nineteenth-century composers as diverse as Field, Schumann, Smetana, Grieg and the master of the miniature, Chopin. As such, it is part of the move away from the German-dominated sonata principle towards the expression of personal, social and nationalistic concerns, and the translation of poetic into musical utterances in small forms like the nocturne, study, prelude or album leaf.

While the appellation 'Album Series' is correct in the sense that the pieces are colourful, some are slight and their structure results from descriptive impulse, it does the work an injustice. *Pictures* is a more coherent whole than Musorgsky suggests. There is the recurring 'Promenade' theme and an overall sense of movement towards the final climax in 'Kiev'. The key-scheme, together with harmonic and motivic characteristics, binds the diverse pieces together and gives them a sense of unity and purpose (see Chapter 4). Furthermore, 'Baba-Yaga' and 'Kiev' are more substantial than album leaves in length and power of expression. It is better to assign *Pictures* to the same genre as piano cycles like Schumann's *Papillons*[3] and *Carnaval*. There are structural parallels between the latter work and *Pictures*. Both contain a sequence of short, simply structured pieces with diverse imagery leading to a lengthier and more triumphant final piece. *Carnaval* lacks any equivalent of Musorgsky's punctuating 'Promenades' but does include a single piece of that title; Musorgsky's motivic links are not as strongly integrating as Schumann's 'ASCH'. Schumann's translation of poetic fantasies and visual images into music was to have a particular attraction for the Russians. Herke introduced Schumann's music to Musorgsky who was among the first of the Russians to appreciate it. Nevertheless, Schumann and Musorgsky are highly divergent. In Musorgsky structure is subordinate to content and Russianness in a way that Schumann's respect for a pure musical language would never allow.

As the nineteenth century progressed a wider range of piano textures became available and standards of performance were improved, matching the composer's need for greater expressive resources. Liszt, who visited St Petersburg in 1842 and 1843, played a crucial role in these developments. Herke's performance of *Totentanz* in 1866 had a strong effect on Musorgsky, and Liszt is the only composer whose piano textures may be traced in *Pictures*. His technique of thematic transformation had an effect too. Other than the faintest traces of Glinka and Balakirev, *Pictures* is remarkably free from the direct influence of other nineteenth-century composers. But in more general terms Musorgsky is a composer of his times in that he is pulled between organicism and the necessities of, in his case, nationalistic and realistic expression with its tendency towards fragmentation and discontinuity. Realistic description in *Pictures* is tempered by the desire for integration through key-schemes, motivic relationships and the recurrences of the 'Promenade' theme. The phrase-structure favours highly periodic two- and four-bar units which then tend to fragment. Romantic too are his interests in folk materials, in delving into the mists of the past, his fascination with the fantastic and his interest in the Jews. However, Musorgsky's feet were firmly anchored in Russian soil; he would not have shared the German Romantic view of the artist as a superhuman, transcendental figure.

Nineteenth-century Russian piano music

The keyboard was the least favoured medium for expressing the nationalistic feelings of the new Russian school. Piano music belonged to the salon or represented Germanic concerns with formalism, development and those things which impeded the creation of a genuinely Russian music. There is little Russian piano music of any substance from the first half of the nineteenth century. Glinka put his energies principally into opera; his contributions to the piano literature are mainly slight mazurkas, waltzes and other salon pieces. Of the composers of the 'Mighty Handful' only Balakirev, a virtuoso pianist, stands out as a composer of piano music developing a 'piano style ... from Hummel, Clementi, Weber and Field to Chopin and Liszt'.[4] His best piano work is the highly idiomatic, unrepentantly virtuosic tone poem for piano *Islamey* (a piece Liszt kept in his repertoire) with its exotic colours, some deriving from Caucasian folk music. Parallelism and modal inflection reflect Balakirev's use of folk music to transform his own musical language. His ornamentation and exotic chromaticism finds little place in Musorgsky's *Pictures*: only in 'Goldenberg' do we find a trace of it. Of Balakirev's other piano music the best dates from after Musorgsky's *Pictures*. Significant piano works by other members of 'The Five', Rimsky-Korsakov's influential Piano Concerto and Borodin's *Petite Suite*, did not appear until the 1880s.

Apart from *Pictures*, Musorgsky's piano music is slight and often derivative, bearing hallmarks of Schumann, Mendelssohn, Balakirev and Chopin.

5

Musorgsky's piano music as a whole is a mixture of travel impressions, comic pieces and scenes from Russian life in much the way that *Pictures* is. Of the early pieces, the *Porte-Enseigne Polka* of 1852 is surprisingly accomplished and pianistic. Better music comes in three Schumannesque pieces from the end of the 1850s. As always Musorgsky improves when scenes and people are involved. The *Impromptu passionné* (1859) is dedicated to his close friend Nadezhda Opochinina and based on two characters in a Herzen novel. *A Children's Prank* (1859) is an early example of Musorgsky writing music on a children's scene. The *Intermezzo* 'in modo classico' (1860–61), a 'post-Schumann pre-Mahler Russianized bucolic Ländler',[5] was later entitled 'A Difficult Path through Snowdrifts', since, as Musorgsky related to Stasov, it was inspired by 'young peasant women, singing and laughing as they walked along an even path' in contrast to other peasants who fell repeatedly into drifts.[6] In 1867 a Trio was added and the piece orchestrated. The piece has an unmistakably Russian theme which is subjected to an uncharacteristically Germanic working-out (hence the 'in modo classico' in the title). Conventional but well written for piano, these three pieces and *The Seamstress* (1871), a rapid, pianistic scherzino, are the best of Musorgsky's piano music other than *Pictures*.

The pieces from the end of his life show a decline in quality. These include two Crimean studies resulting from his tour to southern Russia with the singer Leonova in 1879 (a further piece, *Storm on the Black Sea*, that Musorgsky reputedly played during this tour has either disappeared or was never written down). *Méditation* and *Une Larme* (both 1880) are salon-like album leaves. The famous *Hopak* (also 1880) is a transcription from *Sorochintsy Fair*. *Au village*, his final piece for piano, is more inventive and colourful. Its Russian Orthodox harmonisation of the initially unaccompanied folk-like melody is reminiscent of 'Kiev' and, like most of Musorgsky's late piano music, has traces of Orientalism.

The rich profusion of Russian piano music in the final years of the nineteenth century owes little to Musorgsky's *Pictures*. The line of pianists and pianist-composers that includes Rakhmaninov and Skryabin originated in the establishment of the St Petersburg and, particularly, the Moscow conservatories during the 1860s, and in the work of Anton and Nikolay Rubinstein. During the 1860s and early 70s there was great rivalry between the men of the St Petersburg Conservatory (among whose first graduates were Tchaikovsky and Vasily Bessel, first publisher of *Pictures*) and the Balakirev circle who thought the conservatory training placed too much emphasis on Western techniques and employed too many foreign teachers.[7] But Rimsky-Korsakov's appointment to the St Petersburg Conservatory in 1871 eventually linked the camps. Musorgsky's realistic scene painting would have held little attraction for the new generation of professional, trained musicians who would have considered *Pictures* to be crude and technically flawed. Rakhmaninov and Skryabin were to prefer abstract forms and in Skryabin's later piano music the experimental harmonic language pushed his music towards atonality and expressionism, connecting him more closely with developments in German music than with Musorgsky.

Pictures is a truly Russian work in its directness of expression, its form arising from content and summing of parts rather than organic growth. There is rhythmic drive, excitement, colourfulness; these too are Russian characteristics, as is the use of harmony to support and give colour and weight to lines rather than to control functionally. Musorgsky prefers to depict real life rather than the spiritual, romantic, sensuous or erotic. Less obvious is the need for the listener to probe beneath the surface, to look for concealed layers of meaning, which if not perceived leave the work seeming naive.

Nationalism and Populism

'I feel a certain regeneration; everything Russian seems suddenly near to me.'[8] Musorgsky's oft-quoted words (in a letter to Balakirev 23 June/5 July 1859 describing his reactions to his first visit to Moscow) indicated the onset of nationalism in his music. From then on evocations of Russian scenes in song and opera, and the close imitation of Russian modes of speech formed the backbone of his artistic production. But nationalism is far too broad a term to characterise Musorgsky. He is far from the Czechs Dvořák and Smetana and even from all his compatriots. Not only was his musical language more radical and his rejection of German technique more extensive, but also the subject matter with which he was concerned reflected social and philosophical thought in his country far more than was the case with his contemporaries. So while all the composers of the Balakirev circle and Tchaikovsky may be regarded as nationalists, only Musorgsky intensifies this nationalism by becoming a true popularist and realist. We must look for evidence of all these movements in *Pictures at an Exhibition*.

Musorgsky is often regarded by Soviet commentators as a 'man of the sixties'. In the 1840s and 50s Russian intellectuals had taken two divergent paths towards the establishment of a native culture. The Westernisers (whose musical representatives were Anton Rubinstein and the men of the St Petersburg Conservatory) thought Russians should learn from the West; the

7

Slavophiles thought that they should turn in on themselves and look to native folk culture. In the 1860s and 70s, encouraged by the liberalism of Alexander II (reigned 1855–81) who emancipated the serfs in 1861, the social and philosophical strands first of Nihilism and then Populism were born out of Slavophilism and strongly affected Russian life and thought. Nihilists, like Nikolay Chernyshevsky (1828–89), were anarchistic, but not entirely negative. They were dedicated to freedom and justice and had faith in a better future for all the people.[9] The archetypical Nihilist is Bazarov in Turgenev's *Fathers and Sons*. The novel's Westernising fathers, progressive in their time, were 'too much concerned with generalities, not enough with the specific material evils of the day'.[10] As the Nihilists found their goals, notably self-sufficiency for the peasantry, going unrealised they became frustrated and more extreme, making an attempt on the life of the tsar in 1866 that occasioned a competition for a Great Gate at Kiev.

During the late 1860s Nihilism gave way to Populism, 'a form of agrarian socialism based on a glorification of the Russian ... peasantry'.[11] The peasant commune was seen as a model, and the people, despite their degradations and sufferings, were regarded by the intelligentsia as a source of nobility and morality. Populists like Peter Lavarov (1823–1900) were less materialistic and more inclined to deal with moral, social and historical questions than the Nihilists who simply saw man as a product of biology without a spiritual nature. These essentially left-wing, anti-capitalist movements sought to move Russian life and politics on to a higher political and moral plane. In them lie the seeds of the Russian Revolution and Soviet attitudes to art. Lenin was particularly influenced by Chernyshevsky who was prepared to be exiled, imprisoned or even hanged for his views.

Musorgsky was the only true musical Populist. His music could not be 'classed with any existing group of musicians'[12] and had more in common with Populist intellectuals in other spheres at this time. The emancipation rendered him penniless (he had resigned his commission in 1858) but he bore the common people no malice, and concern and interest in their character and qualities helped shape his unique musical style. *Pictures* is Populistic in its generally positive attitude and in its concern for this world in its various manifestations: work, fantasy, love, comedy, tragedy and death. Even the darkness of 'Catacombs' is mitigated by the illumination of the skulls in 'Con mortuis'. The lives of children and ordinary people in the market place, or fatiguingly driving an ox-cart, are depicted and the composer himself appears promenading around the exhibition. The Russian people sing in 'Kiev', and their folk tales are recalled in 'Baba-Yaga'. Nevertheless, the work is not without darkness and brooding, perhaps indicating a deeper undercurrent of unrest.

Musorgsky considered German music to be overly concerned with an idealistic world only achievable in the abstraction of art-works. In this he reflects the rejection of abstract German thought in the new Russian philosophy. 'Russian speculation (from the 17th century to the post-revolutionary period) has always been decidedly man-centred … [studying] … good and evil in individual and social life, the meaning of individual existence and the nature of history. Russian thinkers turned late and hesitantly, to such disciplines as logic, theory of knowledge and philosophy of science.'[13] On a musical level this indicates that composers should turn their thoughts to life around them rather than to idealistic symphonic development. Such thinking is apparent in 1868 when Musorgsky remarks to Rimsky-Korsakov:

regarding symphonic development. – You seem appalled that you are writing in a Korsakov manner rather than a Schumann manner. … [In] brief, symphonic development, technically understood, is developed by the German, just as his philosophy is…. The German when he thinks first theorises at length and then proves, our Russian brother proves first and then amuses himself with theory.[14]

Pictures is entirely without development in the German sense; it consists of statements and descriptions of characters and personalities in various locations and situations. The length and form of the pieces are dictated by subject matter, not by abstract considerations of symmetry and balance in the service of musical beauty. This and other factors bring us to the artistic product of the new philosophy: realism.

Realism

In 1863 Musorgsky moved into an artistic commune sharing ideas on religion, artistic matters, philosophy and politics with like-minded men in the manner advocated by writer-philosophers such as Belinsky, Herzen and the exiled Chernyshevsky. The latter's *Aesthetic Relationship of Art to Reality* of 1855 was a crucial document in shaping the ideas of the progressive Russian realist writers, artists and their musical representative, Musorgsky. For Chernyshevsky 'true beauty resides in life and the primary purpose of art is to reproduce reality'. In that 'the artist is not simply a passive recorder; in his selection and creation he explains and passes judgement on the reality he portrays, and thus gives his art a moral dimension as well'. Thus we see a 'subordination of aesthetic values to moral and social values'.[15]

'Truth', which in Russian means both veracity and justice, is a key concept in realism. In Musorgsky it relates both to truthful translation of Russian speech-tones into music and truth in depicting Russian life. In his songs and operatic projects his principal concern was to depict with accuracy and to draw almost loving sound portraits of Russian characters and their speech from many walks of life and in widely different situations. Songs like *The Seminarist*, *Yeremushka's Lullaby*, *Kallistrat* and those in *The Nursery* cycle, are all portraits of aspects of Russian life. Vocal music is at the heart of realism; instrumental music was a poor substitute. Musorgsky concentrated his energies, and produced his best and most realistic work, in the spheres of song and opera. In *Pictures* we frequently find him imitating vocal music rather than exploiting the qualities of the piano and we detect a lack of interest in the techniques of instrumental composition. It is arguable that Musorgsky deliberately avoids pianism in *Pictures* considering it, like German harmonic and contrapuntal procedures, routine.

Even without a text, realistic depiction of character types is important in *Pictures* and may be achieved through manner of speech: the shouts of children and their playing rhymes in 'Tuileries', and the contrasting speech character-istics of the two Jews in 'Samuel Goldenberg' (the other meaning of truth as justice is also apparent here). In 'Limoges' we hear various shouts and calls. Placing particular character-types in particular places is very much part of realism: Musorgsky himself at the exhibition, the troubadour in front of the medieval castle, the children in the garden of the Tuileries, the women in the market at Limoges or the masses singing in Kiev.

Musorgsky's most extreme realist work is the incomplete opera *The Marriage* (1868). Influenced by Dargomïzhsky's *The Stone Guest*, Musorgsky attempted to set a text by Gogol verbatim and without compromise for the sake of the music. His intention was to dispense with operatic tradition and express in music human thought and feeling as it takes place in ordinary conversation in a way that was musicianly and artistic: 'an untouched (in the historical course of music) problem – musically to set forth everyday prose in the form of musical prose' (letter to Nikolsky 15/27 August 1868).[16] Although the music sounds unexceptional today, Musorgsky and his friends commented on the strange harmonies this attempt at musical prose seemed to generate. In the end Musorgsky abandoned the project, probably because it was too extreme; realism was jeopardising the artistry of the whole. 'Catacombs' is the nearest we come to musical prose in *Pictures*, and there too we find some of the most extreme harmony and freedom of structure. As a piece on its own 'Catacombs' makes little sense and could hardly even be considered 'artistic' except when placed in context. The other pictures work out the relationship between realistic description and musical structure with rather more equanimity.

A number of other features of musical realism may be identified in *Pictures*. Truth of expression is emphasised over beauty in 'Catacombs', 'Gnomus' and to an extent 'Baba-Yaga'. Unbalanced or dissonant, ugly piano-writing is used to create particular effects, as in the lumbering of the ox-cart in 'Bydlo'. The depiction of motion in music is a feature of realism apparent in Musorgsky shambling round the exhibition, the awkward motion of the gnome, the lumbering cart in 'Bydlo', the fluttering chicks and Baba-Yaga's flight.[17] Stylistic consistency is often compromised by realism. In the musical cartoon *The Classicist* in which Musorgsky attacks a conservatory professor for derogatory remarks he has made about Rimsky-Korsakov's *Sadko*, Musorgsky mixes pastiche eighteenth-century and Rimsky-Korsakov styles in his sarcastic reply. Although *Pictures* is stylistically more consistent and Musorgskian, it nevertheless contains a great diversity of types and lengths of piece.

Realism is more than realistic word- or scene-painting. The descriptive qualities must be linked to real life and usually to social justice. Musorgsky never actively involved himself in politics, but some songs and operatic scenes are critical of the establishment. *The Seminarist* (1866), an open attack on the clerics, was banned from publication by the ecclesiastical censor. *The Forgotten One* (1874) was based on a painting which offended the tsar. Criticism of the historic tsar jeopardised the production of *Boris Godunov*; the revised version of 1874 incorporated sensitive material from Khudiakov's *History*. Khudiakov, who was exiled and had his name suppressed, was one of the group behind the assassination attempt of 1866.[18]

Overtly social and political messages are hard to find in *Pictures*. Soviet commentators, with Musorgsky as a doyen of Soviet realism, read far more into the work than Western listeners. When Fried remarks on the nobility and suffering of the peasant in 'Bydlo' ('the hardships of that patient and persevering toiler') is this fantasy or does the suspicious Russian mind hear a different layer of meaning? Do we take 'Kiev' at its face value or is this, given Musorgsky's Populist leanings and social messages elsewhere in his work, both

11

a celebration of Russian greatness and a veiled reference to the assassination attempt reflecting a more general tendency of realist artists to deal with 'sedition and rebellion'?[19]

Realism is anti-romantic in so far as romanticism implies exaggeration, sentimentality, melodrama and concern with the composer's self-expression over the subject in hand, while the realist artist is always by definition more detached. But it is also very much part of the Romantic age. Musorgsky is its clearest musical adherent, but it is found in other composers' works that deal with deep or violent emotions experienced by everyday people, notably Bizet's *Carmen* or the works of the Italian verismo. As Dahlhaus tells us, realism in music emerged against a background of romanticism's strong survival until the end of the century, after it had ceased to exist in other arts. Indeed, 'Realism was never more than a peripheral phenomenon in the music of the nineteenth century'.[20]

2

Musorgsky and Hartman

Musorgsky in 1874

The year of *Pictures at an Exhibition* was a strange mixture of pessimism and optimism for Musorgsky. Public acclaim came with the staging of *Boris Godunov*; but this was also the year of the desolate, subjective song cycle *Sunless*. The death of Victor Hartman in the previous summer depressed and angered him, and his close friend Nadezhda Opochinina was to die in June 1874. By now drink had a firm hold on Musorgsky; he was prey to bouts of illness and his ability to make sustained efforts at composition was curtailed. But much was still achieved in 1874–5 including extensive work on *Khovanshchina* and *Sorochintsy Fair*, and the *Songs and Dances of Death*. In the end the two operas remained unfinished, but it is wrong to date the decline in his powers as beginning in 1874, as Stasov does. His dogmatic condemnation of the works of this period as 'obscure, mannered, more often incoherent and insipid'[1] is ridiculous and says more about him being annoyed with Musorgsky's drinking and his straying from the path of Russian realism than it does about Musorgsky's work. At this time too, Musorgsky was trying to hold down a full-time, but thoroughly depressing and demoralising, clerical job in the Forestry Department of the Ministry of State Property.

The 'Mighty Handful', despite the efforts of Stasov, was breaking up. Financial pressures had hit the Free Music School and had precipitated Balakirev's withdrawal from musical life until 1876. With the exception of Stasov, Musorgsky was composing free from the influence of his friends; indeed, his relationship with them had become difficult, since they regarded his music as wayward and sometimes illiterate. He was discontented with his fellow composers' idealistic over-concern with technique and tradition and their failure to push at the boundaries of art, something which forced Musorgsky increasingly towards writers, philosophers, visual artists and poets. He formed friendships with the poet Arseny Golenischev-Kutuzov, the sculptor Antokolsky, the painter Repin and the architect Victor Hartman.

13

Musorgsky wanted to depict life, not indulge in the idealistic sonata-form world of the symphonists:

I am not against symphonies, just symphonists, incorrigible conservatives. So don't tell me, dear généralissime, why our musicians talk more about technique than about goals or historical problems .... But one thought still distresses me: Why do the 'Ivans' ... [Statues of Ivan IV and Ivan III on horseback] ... of Antokolsky live? Why do Repin's 'Boatmen' [i.e. the famous Barge-Haulers painting] live? ... Why do the degenerate boy in Perov's 'Birdcatcher' and the first couple in his 'The Hunters' and also ... 'The Village Religious Procession' live? And they live in a way that makes you feel, once you are acquainted with them, that 'you are exactly the one I wanted to see'. Why is it that everything that has been done in the most recent music, despite its excellent qualities, does not live in this way? ... Explain this to me, only leave the boundaries of art aside – I believe in them only relatively because *the boundaries of art* in the religion of an artist mean *stagnation* (letter to Stasov 13/25 July 1872).

The excitement and success of *Boris Godunov*'s staging on 8/20 February 1874 in the Maryinsky Theatre seems to have encouraged Musorgsky in his drinking and what Rimsky refers to as his 'strange ways':

Musorgsky began to appear in our midst somewhat less frequently than before, and a certain change became noticeable in him: he appeared mysterious somehow, perhaps even arrogant. His conceit grew tremendously, and his vague, involved way of expressing himself, which had been characteristic of him, intensified considerably.

On 6/18 March Stasov sent his daughter this portrait of Musorgsky's condition:

he has completely changed. He has begun to drink more and more, his face has swollen and turned dark red, his eyes have gone bad, and he hangs out at the Maly Yaroslavets almost all day, where that damned carousing crowd gathers. So many efforts have been made to drag him out of there and join with all of us again – nothing helps. And besides, he has become somehow petty and pusillanimous.

Orlova, who informs us that the 'Maly Yaroslavets' was in fact quite a respectable establishment, is inclined to think that Stasov may be exaggerating. Certainly Golenischev-Kutuzov's reminiscence (March 1874) of sharing a flat with Musorgsky shows the composer in a quite different light: 'At that time he lived on Shpalernaya, I found two rooms next to him; we opened the doors dividing our lodging so that a small apartment was formed in which we set up our joint housekeeping. All morning until noon (when Musorgsky left for the office) and all evening we spent together in the large room of our house.' Later in the spring Kutuzov wrote to his mother expressing his desire to find a less cramped and warmer apartment. He still hoped that Musorgsky would stay with him, so life could not have been too bad with the alcoholic ex-Guards' officer.[2]

Count Arseny Golenischev-Kutuzov, a descendant of the Kutuzov who commanded the Russian forces against Napoleon in 1812 and who was immortalised in Tolstoy's *War and Peace*, had become a close friend of Musorgsky in 1873 and they had stayed with one another for short periods before moving in together; indeed, there has been speculation that Musorgsky had an unfulfilled homosexual inclination towards him. If speculation that Musorgsky was a masochist with 'a vein of homosexuality'[3] is correct, then his burst of creativity in 1874–5 may well have been stimulated by his close relationship with Golenischev-Kutuzov.

Hartman's death and the composition of *Pictures*

Victor Hartman died on 23 July/4 August 1873 of an aneurism. His early death, at the age of thirty-nine, came just as he reached a point where he might have been able to realise some of his concepts. This utter waste of a talent through early death greatly distressed Musorgsky who also reproached himself for not recognising and acting on the signs of Hartman's fatal condition. If it were not for *Pictures at an Exhibition* Hartman would now be almost completely forgotten. Little if any of his architectural work now remains, and his work as a painter, illustrator and designer is ephemeral. At the time of Hartman's death Stasov was attending the Vienna World Fair where Hartman's model of his National Theatre in Moscow had just earned him a medal. Writing to his sister, Stasov appraised Hartman thus: 'In my eyes he was the most talented, the most original, the most adventurous, the boldest of all our architects, even those of the new young school .... Of course I considered him rather inferior to Musorgsky, Repin and Antokolsky, however, he was a talent – strong!!'.[4]

In Stasov's absence Musorgsky provided an obituary for the *Sankt Peterburgskiye vedemosti* No. 203. The obituary is not an eulogy. Like Stasov, Musorgsky seems to have realised that Hartman was a remarkable talent, but not a genius (despite his reference to Hartman with this term in his autobiography). He points to Hartman's Russianness and social concern, although the only example of the latter is the building of a theatre! Stasov and Count Paul Suzor, president of the Architects' Society, decided to mark Hartman's death with a memorial exhibition of as much of his work as they could gather up. It opened during the second week of February 1874, and ran

15

until March in the Hall of the Academy of Artists in St Petersburg. It contained Hartman's architectural designs (government, military, industrial exhibitions, domestic and so on) and those for craft work, jewellery and ornamentation. Stasov described the exhibition:

One-half of these drawings shows nothing typical of an architect. They are all lively, elegant sketches by a genre-painter, the majority depicting scenes, characters and figures out of everyday life, captured in the middle of everything going on around them: on streets, and in churches, in Parisian catacombs and Polish monasteries, in Roman alleys and in villages around Limoges. There are carnival characters *à la* Gavarni, workers in smocks, priests with umbrellas under their arms riding mules, elderly French women at prayer, Jews smiling from under their skull caps, Parisian rag-pickers ... landscapes with scenic ruins, magnificently done with a panorama of the city .... Architecture fills the other half of his drawings.[5]

He goes on to describe Hartman's project for a Great Gate at Kiev in detail (see Chapter 5).

Stasov notes the genre-painter's mixture of characters and nationalities and typically draws attention to Hartman's scenes from everyday life. The sketches are regarded as 'lively and elegant' but do not merit the critic's detailed attention in the way that the genuinely Russian nationalistic project for the Great Gate does. Of the four hundred works by Hartman exhibited, less than one hundred have ever come to light. The situation has been confused by extra items being added to the exhibition as it progressed but not listed in the catalogue.[6] Only six of the designs and illustrations that directly relate to *Pictures* may be identified with certainty (see Chapter 5).

'Musorgsky, who loved Hartman passionately and was deeply moved by his death, planned to "draw in music" the best pictures of his deceased friend, representing himself as he strolled through the exhibition, joyfully or sadly recalling the highly talented deceased artist (Promenade).'[7] There is no record of when Musorgsky visited the exhibition, or exactly when he conceived the idea of his musical tribute. Stasov claimed in a letter of 1903 to Arkady Kerzin that he made suggestions as to the content of the work. There is no evidence to support this, beyond the close relationship between the two men and the way in which they constantly discussed Musorgsky's projects. It is possible that Stasov had a hand in shaping *Pictures* as he did by suggesting the scenes for the *Songs and Dances of Death* (1875).

The manuscript of *Pictures* was prepared in about twenty days (approximately 2–22 June O. S.), providing further evidence that Musorgsky's mind was clear at this time. The final page of the manuscript is dated '22 June 1874

16

St Petersburg'; a few days of tidying-up must then have followed (when some of the small alterations may have been made) before the dedication to Stasov dated 27 June 1874 was added and the half-erased remark in blue pencil: 'For press. Musorgsky, 26 July 1874'. There are no sketches and little information about its composition. In general, Musorgsky composed at the piano and tended only to produce a finished score; usually he was able to play complete compositions, or substantial portions of them, well in advance of the date of the manuscript.

Orlova suggests that Musorgsky improvised or sketched *Pictures* during the spring: 'judging from the correspondence between Rimsky-Korsakov and Stasov, Musorgsky had already played the first half of the suite in the spring. ... [In June] Musorgsky polished the first half of the work, composed the second half and wrote out the entire piece'.[8] Orlova's idea was presumably prompted by Stasov's remark to Rimsky-Korsakov: 'You don't know the second part at all' (in a letter quoted more fully below). However, it is hard to see how Rimsky-Korsakov could have actually heard any of *Pictures* earlier in the year since he was away from St Petersburg training a military band from before the Hartman exhibition; any knowledge he had of it was more likely to have come from Stasov.

Musorgsky's letter to Stasov (probably 12/24 June) gives the impression of a composer working at white heat:

Hartman is boiling as Boris boiled; sounds and ideas have been hanging in the air; I am devouring them and stuffing myself – I barely have time to scribble them on paper. I am writing the fourth number – the links are good (on 'promenade'). I want to finish it as quickly and securely as I can. My profile can be seen in the interludes. I consider it successful to this point .... The titles are curious: 'Promenade (in modo russico)'. No. 1, 'Gnomus' – intermezzo (the intermezzo is untitled); No. 2, 'Il vecchio castello' – intermezzo (also untitled); No. 3, 'Tuileries' (*dispute enfants après jeux*); right between the eyes, No. 4, 'The Sandomirsko Bydlo' (*le télègue*) (*le télègue*, obviously is untitled, which is between us). How well it is working out ... I want to add Vityushka's [i.e. Victor Hartman's] Jews.

How long or in what state these ideas had been hanging in the air is unclear from this, the only reference to *Pictures at an Exhibition* in Musorgsky's prodigious correspondence. There is the strong impression that Musorgsky was trying to keep himself at it, trying to work in a controlled manner without, presumably, alcoholic diversions; his culinary references are typical. How much of the overall structure he had in mind when he began is difficult to tell. The letter above suggests he worked at the opening five pieces in order and was about to add the sixth. Whether he had fully formulated ideas for the other pieces is not clear, but we do get the impression that the work was composed in its final sequence.

The second half of *Pictures* is described in a letter from Stasov to Rimsky-Korsakov:

Musoryanin has positively completed and written the last stroke of his piece on Hartman. The *second part* you don't know at all, and there, I think are the very best things. 'The Limoges Gossips at the Market' – an enchanting scherzino and very pianistic. Then comes 'Baba-Yaga' – excellent and powerful, and in conclusion – 'The Kiev Bogatyr's Gate' – in the manner of a hymn or finale *à la* 'Slavsiya' – of course a million times worse and weaker, but all the same a lovely, mighty and original thing. There is a particularly lovely church motif: 'As you are baptised in Christ', and the ringing bells are in a completely new style. In this second part are a few unusually poetic lines. This [musical quotation] is the music for Hartman's picture of the 'Catacombs of Paris' all made of skulls. Musoryanin has begun with a depiction of a gloomy vault (long stretched chords, purely orchestral, with great [pause mark]). Then tremolando comes in a minor key the theme of the first promenade, – these are faint lights glimmering in the skulls, and here suddenly is sounded the magic, poetical appeal of Hartman to Musorgsky.[9]

Stasov's tone is slightly derogatory: 'Kiev' is not the equal of the hallowed Glinka's 'Slavsiya'. But in presenting Musorgsky's music to those outside the circle he would be more positive. He reported to Tchaikovsky in September 1874 that Musorgsky has composed 'six new romances, of which two are absolutely first rate, and a large piano piece ... which is unusually original, powerful and refined'.

Musorgsky's operatic projects took years to bring to fruition. The successful completion of *Pictures* in an extraordinary bout of concentrated activity indicates that the scale of the work, as with his songs, was commensurate with his ability to sustain concentration. Had he delayed but a week things might have been different. On the 29 June/11 July Nadezhda Opochinina (*b.* 1821) died. Opochinina was the sister of Alexander and Vladimir Opochinin. Musorgsky had lived with the Opochinin family during the composition of *Boris* and Alexander had assisted Musorgsky in finding government employment on several occasions. Musorgsky's relationship with Nadezhda Opochinina is, like his relationships with women in general and his absolute horror of marriage, something of a mystery. Nadezhda was eighteen years his senior but a large number of significant compositions are dedicated to her and Musorgsky did not make his dedications lightly. No correspondence exists to help us establish their relationship.

The work of Victor Hartman

Partly because of his early death, the architect Victor Alexandrovich Hartman[10] is a rather minor figure in Russian art and there is little evidence that his life was the passionate struggle some Soviet commentators have suggested.[11] Indeed, the opposite was the case. He seems to have lived a comfortable, untroubled existence, able to travel throughout Europe from 1864 to 1868 indulging himself in his penchant for making water colours and sketches of cathedrals and buildings of architectural interest, and the scenes from life that inspired Musorgsky. Little or nothing of Hartman's elaborate architecture now remains; Mamontov the publisher's country house (now demolished) was typical of his architectural style. The roofs were steeply pitched and surmounted with elaborate filigree work as were the fascias. The symmetry inherent in this jewellery-type decoration, in the steep-pitched roofs and in the elaborately decorated dormer windows, was offset by the asymmetry of the building itself with its almost haphazardly placed little wings and porches. As the realist artist Kramskoy remarked: 'When he was to build commonplace, utility objects Hartman was a failure, for he needed fairy-tale castles and fantastic palaces for which there were no precedents – here he could create truly wonderful things'.[12]

Hartman produced a number of fantastic, almost impractical designs for everyday items such as that for a nutcracker, which inspired 'Gnomus', and the design for a clock in the form of Baba-Yaga's hut on hen's legs. Frankenstein was also able to trace Hartman's designs for a presentation jug in the form of a chicken standing on a single clawed foot, and a candelabrum.[13] Reflecting the qualities of nature, Hartman mixes regular and irregular, taking asymmetrical shapes and either drawing out or adorning them with patterns and symmetries. Sometimes this can have a glib effect, as with the two chickens' heads placed in mirror image at the top of Baba-Yaga's clock or the sawtooth pattern of the cock's comb on the top of the presentation jug which connects with diamond shapes used in other additions. On the other hand, the plaited, snake-like strands of varying thicknesses on the upper part of the plinth of the clock are better.

Musorgsky befriended Hartman in 1870. That year he dedicated 'In the Corner' from *The Nursery* to Hartman who advocated performing the songs with sets and costumes; it was Hartman who prevailed on the composer to restore the fountain scene in *Boris Godunov*. Minds of the stature of Musorgsky and Stasov were attracted to Hartman's work by the Russianness that veneered it, whether derived from peasant embroidery or country life in the form of bird and animal motifs. The chickens that appear so frequently played a crucial role in the rural economy. The composer and the critic were also struck by the originality and quality of his artistry; the ordinariness of the materials or the subject did not matter. But it is clear that Hartman's work lacked the strong Populist/realist social commitment of Musorgsky's music.

Social comment is difficult to incorporate in architecture or design, but even Hartman's sketches and watercolours seem substantially unaffected by the Populist and realist movements. It would have been convenient for Soviet musicologists had Victor Hartman been one of the Russian realist artists or 'Peredvizniki'. This movement was 'born of protest in 1863 and died of senility in 1923'; only ten years later it was resurrected for political reasons as 'the basis for Socialist Realism. And until recently this style flourished in the Soviet Union'.[14] But Hartman's name does not crop up amongst those of painters Ivan Kramskoy (1837–87), Vasili Perov (1833–82), Ilya Repin, and sculptor Mark Antokolsky (1842–1902). Hartman was a man of the sixties only in so far as he was part of the Slavonic renaissance in architecture, which sought inspiration in folk materials. Musorgsky's social concerns and realism place him a long way from Hartman's ephemeral sketches, and his musical style, stripped of all ornament, contrasts with Hartman's fussiness. But as well as their interest in things Russian and in scenes from life there is a deeper link in that both men's work often suggests realisation in other media and may give an impression of incompleteness. Both seem to be working in media only partly able to cope with what they wish to express. Furthermore, with both we must tolerate a certain slightness in the individual items and only come to a judgement in the context of the whole musical suite or exhibition. In the end, Musorgsky is a much more fundamentally Russian artist than Hartman.

3

Manuscript, publication and performance

Currently musicologists and performers take faithfulness to the original text and the use of performance practices from the composer's day as benchmarks of good musical practice. There is a marked reluctance to admit that a composer worth performing can possibly be improved upon; indeed, there is often the feeling that a composer's originality and strength lies in those passages which may previously have been considered to be flawed. Musorgsky's music raises this authenticity issue in a nineteenth-century context. While so many musicians have tried to 'improve him' in the past there is now a counter-effort to establish reliable texts for works such *Pictures* and *Boris Godunov*, a quest not helped during the early decades of this century by the arrival of an unreliable complete edition by Paul Lamm.

The manuscript

The only manuscript of *Pictures*, in Musorgsky's hand, is preserved in the manuscripts' department of the Saltykov–Schedrin Public Library in St Petersburg. A title page and twenty-five pages of score take up the bulk of a little book comprising eight double sheets of manuscript paper sewn together. Musorgsky's ink calligraphy is clear and has few errors. Alterations and corrections are made in pencil or by scraping-out the offending notes with a sharp edge and then inking-in new ones. Some larger-scale cuts and alterations are indicated by dense crossings-out or by Musorgsky covering the unwanted text with strips of new manuscript tied to each margin. In all cases where Musorgsky has made an alteration it is possible to study both old and new versions. A small number of facsimiles of the autograph were produced in 1975.[1]

Musorgsky's manuscript requires only slight editorial efforts. Sometimes where his slurs begin and end is unclear; his use of staccato marks is a little ambiguous or inconsistent; some accidentals are missing but context makes it quite clear what they should be. Musorgsky makes a couple of slips in the notation of rhythm in 'Tuileries' and some editors have had difficulties with the rhythmic notation in 'Goldenberg'.

Although Musorgsky wrote 'for press' on the bottom right-hand corner of the title page of the autograph on 26 July/7 August 1874, just one month after the completion of the work, there is no evidence to suggest that any publisher was interested in the manuscript. He may well have fantasised about the success of his pieces and their appeal.

Two days before his death Musorgsky, at Stasov's behest, appointed T. I. Filippov, an admirer and government official, as his executor. On Musorgsky's death Filippov quickly arranged for Bessel to acquire, without fee, the rights to all of Musorgsky's unpublished works, among them *Pictures*. Bessel had shown interest in Musorgsky's music during his lifetime, having enough faith to publish a vocal score of the second version of *Boris Godunov* before it was accepted for performance. Rimsky-Korsakov was given the job of editing the scores and thus began one of the major controversies in musical history:

I undertook to set in order and complete all of Musorgsky's works and turn over gratis to the Bessel firm those that I should find suitable for the purpose. For the next year and a half or two years my work on my dead friend's compositions went on. [Musorgsky's manuscripts] were in exceedingly imperfect order; there occurred absurd, incoherent harmonies, ugly part-writing, ... illogical modulation, ... ill-chosen instrumentation ... in general; a certain audacious self-conceited dilettantism, at times moments of technical dexterity and skill but more often of utter technical impotence ... publication without a skilful hand to put them in order would have had no sense save a biographical-historical one. If Musorgsky's compositions are destined to live unfaded for fifty years after their author's death (when all his works will become the property of any and every publisher), such an archeologically accurate edition will always be possible, as the manuscripts went to the Public Library on leaving me.[2]

These remarks, while undoubtedly directed at Musorgsky's operatic projects rather than *Pictures*, show Rimsky-Korsakov to have an attitude to authenticity quite opposed to that prevailing today. Furthermore, Rimsky-Korsakov had, just a few years before, immersed himself in the study of harmony and counterpoint and had a much higher regard for technique than Musorgsky. However, we may safely conclude from the limited extent of his revisions that he considered *Pictures* to be among the least reprehensible of Musorgsky's manuscripts. Rimsky-Korsakov tells us nothing of his work on *Pictures*, undoubtedly considering it one of his friend's less consequential works. He duly delivered it to Bessel who published it in 1886, adding Stasov's famous remarks as a preface.

The impression, encouraged by Rimsky-Korsakov, that every piece Musorgsky wrote was flawed, full of silly errors and in places unacceptably ugly, is widespread. Unable until recently to see the manuscript, scholars probably thought Rimsky-Korsakov's editorial work on *Pictures* to have been more extensive than it was, giving rise to the view that his version is more unreliable and distorted than it actually is. Alfred Kreuz's remark that the 'first editors of the work thought it wiser not to print the harsh harmonies which would have sounded too daring for that time' is arrant nonsense.[3] Even in 1984 Manfred Schandert cannot resist a snipe at Rimsky-Korsakov 'who – with the best of intentions – felt obliged to amend some of Musorgsky's more daring touches'. Rimsky-Korsakov's amendments have little to do with Musorgsky's daring touches, and more to do with Rimsky-Korsakov himself adding further effects and tidying up things that he misunderstood or misread in Musorgsky's autograph.

Rimsky-Korsakov's editorial practice, with just a few glaring exceptions, was relatively restrained. The principal distortion was replacing Musorgsky's *fortissimo* marking at the beginning of 'Bydlo' with '*pp*', and a 37-bar *poco-a-poco* crescendo occupying over half of the piece which Ravel used to brilliant effect in his orchestration. The other major imperfection was the omission of some *attacca* markings. Much of his tidying up was unexceptional involving minor adjustments to phrasing, dynamics and articulation. Changes of harmony were few; the bold dissonances in 'Catacombs' were left alone. In 'Limoges' (bar 27, left hand) an Eb/G is substituted for Musorgsky's D/F; thus the bar and the return to the theme begin with a tonic rather than a dominant chord (Rimsky-Korsakov may have felt a V–I strong/weak harmonic rhythm to be unsatisfactory at the beginning of a new section).[4]

Rimsky-Korsakov misread Musorgsky's rhythm in the first bar of 'Goldenberg'. He turned the composer's three semiquavers at the beginning of the fourth beat into a triplet (Ravel's orchestration has made Rimsky's triplet so familiar that Musorgsky's original sounds unsettling), but he failed to compensate by doubling the final two note-values, leaving the bar short of a semiquaver. Tampering with Musorgsky's semiquavers at the beginning of the fourth beat destroys the rhythmic concordance between the upward moving A–Bb–C figures on the fourth beats of bars 1, 2 and 4. Rimsky-Korsakov also doubles the length of the upbeat to bar 7 (presumably because Musorgsky failed to double-dot the rest before this note in the manuscript), thus ruining the consistency of Goldenberg's upbeats. As Edward Reilly points out, subsequent editions, prior to our recommended Urtext, fail to sort this out.[5]

There are odd moments when one feels Rimsky-Korsakov's alterations might be right. In 'Gnomus' (bar 34) he alters Musorgsky's C♭ (second quaver) to B♭, paralleling bar 9. In Schandert's 'Urtext', the C♭ is restored, but it remains a fair bet that Musorgsky made a mistake here. Rimsky-Korsakov's edition was marred as much by silly typographical errors as by wilful editorial practice: there are missing dynamics, accidentals and some wrong notes.[6] Bessel translated the Russian title and those of the final two pieces into French. 'The Bogatyr [Knight's] Gate (at Kiev, the Ancient Capital)' becomes 'The Great Gate at Kiev'. Otherwise Musorgsky's important multi-language titles were not interfered with. The title 'Promenade' was given to the untitled second, third and fourth returns of the opening idea (Musorgsky called them intermezzos), but Musorgsky's notation without key signatures is preserved in these pieces.

The Bessel edition, and its German sister produced by Breitkopf & Härtel, were all that was available to editors and performers until the volume of solo piano music was added to the complete edition in 1939. Unfortunately, while the complete edition dealt with some of Rimsky-Korsakov's transgressions, such as the wrong dynamic at the head of 'Bydlo', it failed to clear up errors such as the rhythmic confusion at the beginning of 'Goldenberg' and it retained some inaccurate titles. In consequence, editions derived from this, notably the 'Urtexts' of Alfred Kreuz (1954) and Alexander Borovsky (1957), are imperfect. Only since 1975, with the availability of the facsimile autograph and more scholarly attitudes to musicology, has it been possible to produce true Urtexts, Manfred Schandert's being the best; Cristoph Hellmundt's is marred by his failure to tackle properly the rhythmic problems in 'Goldenberg'.

One of the most interesting early editions was edited by O. Thümer and published in London in 1914. While close to Rimsky-Korsakov in some respects, Thümer seems to have corrected errors in the Rimsky-Korsakov version which are not obvious without access to the original autograph. Although it is unlikely that Thümer consulted the manuscript directly, he is likely to have known the work of the English scholars of Russian music, M. Montagu-Nathan and Rosa Newmarch (the latter worked with Stasov in the St Petersburg Library during the late 1890s). Montagu-Nathan published articles and lectured on Musorgsky about the time of the Augener edition. He may well have drawn Thümer's attention to the metronome markings supplied in a letter from Stasov to Arkady Kerzin, since his is the first edition to contain them.[7] Despite the current mistrust of these early twentieth-century English editions Thümer's editorial practice is restrained and this is the most accurate of the early editions.

The rash of Urtexts over the last thirty years corresponds to the rash of orchestral transcriptions. The ever greater sins perpetrated against the work by orchestrators seems to have generated a counter-force seeking to find the definitive original text with ever greater zeal but never quite achieving its goal.

Performances

No record of a public performance of *Pictures* during Musorgsky's lifetime exists. That Musorgsky must have played the pieces to Stasov and Rimsky-Korsakov is clear from their letters and from their attempts to remember Musorgsky's tempos. Strangely, Musorgsky did not include it in the pieces he performed on his tour in 1879. In its original piano version, *Pictures* appears to have crept into the repertoire rather than taken it by storm. The first record of a public performance of *Pictures* is of Touschmaloff's partial orchestration on 30 November 1891. According to Montagu-Nathan, Arkady Kerzin, an early biographer of Musorgsky and leader of a circle of lovers of Russian music in Moscow, did try to arrange a piano performance in 1903, and it was for this occasion that Stasov and Rimsky-Korsakov tried to recall the metronome marks. If this performance did take place it may well have been amongst the earliest public ones.

There must have been some sales of Bessel's 1886 publication and Augener's of 1914. We can safely assume that most of these were to enthusiastic amateurs and connoisseurs of Russian music who would put them to their own private use. In the years immediately preceding the advent of gramophone recordings the appetite for piano music for the parlour was voracious. It is quite probable that the easier pictures would be better known there than in the concert hall and that these were often played on their own to the detriment of the overall conception. The fantastic, colourful nature of Musorgsky's piano work would have appealed as did the album leaves of other composers. The first English performance of the complete work, at a lecture by Montagu-Nathan at the Musical Association, came in December 1914, coinciding with the arrival of the Augener Edition. The performances given at Kerzin's circle and Montagu-Nathan's lecture both tend to suggest that *Pictures* was considered to be out of the ordinary, with at least some curiosity value. Even in Russia it was not generally taken up by pianists of the virtuosic line from the Moscow Conservatory until well into the twentieth century, presumably because they regarded it as unpianistic and technically weak.

Sir Henry Wood's orchestration (1915) and particularly that by Maurice Ravel (1922) were the real catalysts in promoting interest in the work; but the

25

interest tended to focus on the orchestral versions, which, as described later, gradually grew in number as the years went by. The orchestral versions eclipsed the original which came to be regarded as little more than a sketch. A notorious series of airings of the piano version which reflected this attitude was given by Vladimir Horowitz, the most famous occasion being the Carnegie Hall performance in April 1951, preserved on record.[8] Horowitz considerably adulterates Musorgsky's score in his performance; his intention seems to be to convert Ravel's orchestration into a piano work rather than to return to Musorgsky's original.

The lack of recordings of the piano version until the 1940s is symptomatic of its neglect. To my knowledge, the earliest recording is that by Alexander Brailowsky made in 1942. This was followed by those of Benno Moiseiwitsch in 1947 and Horowitz's first recording (in his own version of the work) made in 1948.[9] All these performances are of course by Russian exile pianists. Only with more performances by Russians could the power of the work's conception be revealed. Unfortunately, the restrictions placed on travel by the Soviet government, notably during Stalin's regime, prevented these. It is fair to conclude from performances of the work given in the West when the travel restrictions eased and there came an influx of Russian pianists in the 1960s, that performances of Musorgsky's 'realistic' masterpiece became more frequent in his native land as the century progressed and that the work came to be exalted in musical journals and books. It was a pity that this model of 'Social Realism' was not displayed for the reform of the decadent West until it was nearly a century old! The passion and quality of these Soviet performances was clearly illustrated by one given by Sviatoslav Richter in Sofia in February 1958, preserved on record. Richter's performance, while not definitive, is a landmark in the history of *Pictures*.[10]

Recordings of Ravel's orchestral version actually predate those of the piano version. Sergey Koussevitzky, who had commissioned Ravel to make his transcription, made his famous recording with the Boston Symphony Orchestra in 1930. Melichar recorded it with the Berlin State Orchestra in 1931 (one reviewer, in the *Gramophone*, compared it with Sir Henry Wood's orchestration, which he said was the most commonly performed at that time). As recording techniques improved, Ravel's and to some extent Stokowski's orchestration took on the dubious role of test pieces for recording techniques and hi-fi systems. Indeed, this work must be one of the most frequently recorded in the catalogues. That so many people have come to know it in the colourful Ravel version recorded in glowing hi-fi sound has promoted negative attitudes to the more monochrome piano version, particularly amongst those who listen to the piece purely as a sonic experience rather than both for the music and the messages from nineteenth-century Russia.

From the mid-1950s increasing numbers of pianists, including Katchen, Pennario and Brendel have taken up the challenge of *Pictures*. The Russian pianist Vladimir Ashkenazy has been particularly closely associated with the piece, and as well as collaborating on the Vienna Urtext Edition has also produced an orchestration. His recording in the late 1960s was a milestone in that it attempted to get as close as possible to the original. The degree to which Rimsky-Korsakov's piano version and Ravel's orchestration had implanted themselves on the minds of listeners is clear from the remarks of an anonymous reviewer in 1968 who expressed his surprise at the insertion of an extra 'Promenade' and criticises Ashkenazy thus: '"Bydlo" starts off much too loudly; it is marked "*p*"'![11]

The success of any performance of *Pictures* that is true to the composer's intentions will ultimately rest on the vividness with which the scenes are evoked, the extent to which the inherent Russianness is brought to the fore, the balance struck between the comic, serious, pantomimic and lyrical elements and, finally, the way in which the performer perceives and presents the underlying unifying elements within the work. But these rules of thumb are often overridden by orchestrators, transcribers and performers less concerned with meanings than with sonic display.

4

Looking at Musorgsky's 'Pictures at an Exhibition'

In this part of the book we turn our attention to the score of *Pictures*. But, with this work more than many others, it is meaningless just to subject it to musical analysis since it is so deeply connected with the composer's life, artistic philosophies and preoccupations. In recent years music analysts have tended to avoid works with a high degree of external reference, so it is hardly surprising that *Pictures* has rarely been the subject of analysis. Quite apart from the specifics of the music, Musorgsky's score is a remarkable document. He employs no less than six languages (Russian, French, Italian, Polish, Yiddish/German and Latin). Titles are chosen with great care, with even the punctuation being significant. The linguistic capability reflects Musorgsky's command of European languages. Shifting style according to expressive necessity is very much part of his literary technique. When he wrote texts in Russian for songs and operas, his language changed according to the type of character being depicted, something that also happens in the music. For Musorgsky expression and characterisation come before the beauty and consistency of the literary text. The exact titles of pieces and the little comments that Musorgsky appends in several places are all of significance. What Harold Bauer did in his 'transcription' of the piece in freely translating the titles into a kind of rootless, nationless Anglo–American is wrong because it necessarily removes a whole layer of meaning from the text which must act as an invaluable guide to the performer.

Study of the manuscript reveals Musorgsky striving to find the best titles and guides to the programmatic content of his pictures. The title 'Bydlo', for example, is written over a never-to-be-discovered erased predecessor. The title of the ballet remains in pencil as though Musorgsky was not too sure about it. He makes two attempts at providing a programme for 'Limoges' and then abandons both. He would like a little bit of Latin prose to connect 'Catacombs' and 'Con mortuis', but his Latin was not quite up to it. What all this indicates is that the precise title is important: he was striving for a precision of nomenclature to match the precise musical conception.

Stasov's remarks on the individual pictures are well known and have come to be printed in many of the editions, either wholly or partially, exactly translated or paraphrased. These remarks can be rather confusing because they emanate from three sources. They first appear as a footnote in Stasov's biography of Musorgsky published in two parts in *The European Herald* (1881; the way that this information is given as a footnote indicates the peripheral importance Stasov gave to the work).[1] Then come Stasov's remarks in the Bessel edition of the score (1886); finally there are remarks from Stasov in a letter to Arkady Kerzin in 1903. This last source adds little new; its principal interest is that it provides a number of metronome markings (mentioned in Chapter 3). These recollections by Stasov, written down after a substantial lapse of time, are sometimes at variance with Musorgsky's notes in the manuscript and with his letter of June 1874 in which he described the pieces (see above p. 18). Stasov clearly made his remarks from memory; for example, he does not mention that the children are in dispute in 'Tuileries', nor are the two Jews named. These wrong titles found their way into such important sources on Musorgsky as Leyda and Bertensson who give as the titles 'on the manuscript' not those that are actually there, but those of the first published edition.[2] In Chapter 5 I therefore give Musorgsky's full titles as they appear in the manuscript, preserving their original languages and their use of inverted commas. If every detail is preserved, we can almost hear Musorgsky pronouncing these titles.

Musorgsky's use of musical notation is also interesting. His markings are often extravagant (notably that at the head of the first 'Promenade'), but they are meaningful and reflect a desire to convey his intentions accurately. The manuscript is carefully marked in regard to phrasing and articulation. Double bar-lines are not used at changes of time signature but appear in most pieces as indicators of structural divisions. 'Promenades' 2–4 are notated without key signatures, which carries a message about their transitory nature and their roles as intermezzos.

With regard to the use of the piano we find lines, usually shorn of ornament and figuration, stylistically remote from those of the most celebrated nineteenth-century pianist-composers. Even such a straightforward device as the arpeggio is virtually absent. The idea of spinning out a harmony with figuration seemed, to Musorgsky, to be an unnecessary indulgence in purely musical activity. Where figuration is used it is almost invariably scalic. Only at the end of 'Limoges' and 'Baba-Yaga' does he indulge in outbursts of rapid

Lisztian figuration. Even simple ornaments such as the trill are rarely used and are reserved for effects rather than decoration (for example, the fluttering of feathers in 'Chicks').

Demands on the pianist are often more a matter of awkwardness than virtuosity and much of the music seems to be conceived for voice (either solo: 'Castello' and 'Bydlo'; or chorus: 'Promenade' and the chorales in 'Kiev'), brass ('Catacombs' and 'Kiev'), woodwind and bells. In 'Castello' the pianist is also given the ungrateful task of reiterating a G♯ pedal for 107 bars so as to give the impression of a guitar strumming in the background. Not that moments of real pianism are not present, particularly in 'Tuileries' and 'Limoges' with their high sparkling writing. But the registration is generally deeper, with emphasis on the lower registers both in melodic writing and chordal layout. While this is often to create a particular effect, as in 'Catacombs' and 'Bydlo', it also results from the Russian tendency towards darkness and melancholy. In general there is an unpianistic tendency to use full chords moving in a quick harmonic rhythm. The full inner parts, as in 'Promenade', may detract from the melodic line. While we might associate fullness of sound with *Pictures* there is a surprising amount of monodic and non-imitative two-part writing. Pedalling is only marked in Musorgsky's autograph in Nos. 6, 9 and 10. While judicious use of the pedal might be appropriate elsewhere, the nature of the music is such that it requires sharpness and clarity, with distinct rather than blurred changes of harmony.

Pictures into music: the structure of the whole

Musorgsky's music thrives on striking a balance between realistic expression and the exigencies of proper, artistic musical construction. The overall structure of *Pictures* must be approached both from the purely musical angle, and from the point of view of the subject-matter. Music like this is to some extent narrative and will tolerate a higher level of structural freedom (and even imperfection). Nevertheless, purely musical structuring is by no means disregarded in *Pictures*.

Examples of composers being directly inspired by particular works of visual art are quite rare. One thinks of Liszt's 'Sposalizio' and 'Il penseroso' from the *Années de pèlerinage*, Stravinsky's *The Rake's Progress*, Respighi's *Trittico botticelliano* and Vaughan Williams's *Job*. The broader links between Debussy and the Impressionist painters, and Schoenberg and the Expressionists also come to mind. The reasons why few such links exist owe much to the lack of a time dimension in painting. A composer like Musorgsky needs narrative;

his creativity may be stimulated by a moment encapsulated in a picture, but he then needs to wrap the picture in a sequence of events. For each little Hartman illustration, Musorgsky the opera and song composer creates a little story.

Musorgsky tends to focus on something or somebody depicted within the picture rather than being directly concerned with the art-work itself. In 'Gnomus' he is more interested in the stumbling gnome than the nutcracker, in 'Baba-Yaga' more in witches than clocks, in 'Castello' more in the troubadour than the castle. Goldenberg and Schmuÿle must engage in an argument, and in 'Limoges' Musorgsky actually began to pencil in the words of the various disputants in the market. Thus he is able to exploit the narrative potential in Hartman's sketches and designs. Hartman can show us the insides of the catacombs and portray the lines of skulls; only Musorgsky can convey the eerie impression of them gradually lighting up. Music has the power to express what may be latent in other art-forms, just as it may transcend and add new layers of meaning to the text set in a song. But only the illustrations themselves can actually encapsulate the scene, character or item at the heart of the music. It almost goes without saying that this high degree of complementarity indicates that the true richness of the musical composition can only be appreciated if we know something about the pictures, their subject-matter and the concerns of late nineteenth-century Russian artists.

The composer wandering round the exhibition from picture to picture creates a minimal narrative structure for the whole work; but the blend of moods and episodes in *Pictures* has the external qualities of a narrative without actually being one. In some ways it represents a trip through life without an overall story or plot. In its mixture of the fantastic ('Gnomus' and 'Baba-Yaga'), the comic ('Chicks'), social comment ('Goldenberg'), love ('Castello') and religion ('Kiev') it has many of the ingredients of a good story. While it reflects the mixture of these elements and the trivial and grandly architectural in the work of Hartman, Musorgsky puts more emphasis on people. The work also focuses on both the ancient and the modern.

An important question about this work is the extent to which the order of the individual pieces is immutable. There is an underlying key-scheme, described below, which does not bear much modification (a point not recognised by most of the arrangers including Ravel who leaves out a crucial 'Promenade'). However, more important than the key-scheme is the best sequence from the point of view of balancing comic and serious, lyric and pantomimic, fast and slow, weighty and less weighty. Determining the best and most satisfying sequence is, to an extent, beyond analysis except in the general sense that it is best to end, as Musorgsky does, with the weightiest and most powerfully Russian pieces: 'Baba-Yaga' and 'Kiev', the latter with its climactic, ceremonial reference to the 'Promenade' theme.

The Soviet musicologist Bobrovsky has suggested that the subject-matter can be symmetrically arranged with 'Chicks' at the centre (see Figure 1):[3]

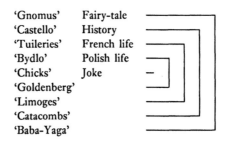

'Gnomus'	Fairy-tale
'Castello'	History
'Tuileries'	French life
'Bydlo'	Polish life
'Chicks'	Joke
'Goldenberg'	
'Limoges'	
'Catacombs'	
'Baba-Yaga'	

Figure 1

While this scheme has some merit, the idea that 'Chicks', one of the slenderest pieces in the set, should have a pivotal role is obviously weak, as is the notion that 'Kiev' is a kind of appendage outside the symmetrical scheme (although arguably 'Promenade' and 'Kiev' could be considered as framing the whole). The plan is lent credence by the distinct tonal break between 'Bydlo' and 'Chicks'. Another way of looking at the blend of moods and episodes in much of the work is to pair the pieces into dark and low/light and high: 'Castello'/ 'Tuileries', 'Bydlo'/'Chicks', 'Goldenberg'/'Limoges', 'Catacombs'/'Con Mortuis'.

We must beware of pushing this kind of thinking too far, in many ways the structure of *Pictures* is rather like the structure of an art exhibition: there are stronger and weaker ways of arranging the materials, but no ideal way. Indeed, just as an exhibition is held together by the style of the artist who is being exhibited, so this work is held together by the style of its composer.[4]

As I have stressed, there are two aspects to the overall structure, the arrangement of the materials according to their moods and substance and the musical structure reflected in keys and themes. As Figure 2 indicates, E♭ is the principal tonic. Not only is it the key of the final picture, but it is also a common denominator: the tonal region to which all the other keys best relate. With enharmonic conversions, most of the keys in the piece are diatonic to E♭ major or minor. The sequence of keys clearly divides in two. The succession of fifths and relatives is broken by the diminished fifth shift to D minor at the opening of 'Promenade' 5 which then moves to F for 'Chicks'. Another

			in E♭ major/minor	locally
1st	'Promenade'	B♭ major	V	
No. 1	'Gnomus'	E♭ minor	i	v
2nd	'Promenade'	A♭ major	IV	I
No. 2	'Castello'	G♯ minor	iv	i/vi
3rd	'Promenade'	B major	♭VI	I
No. 3	'Tuileries'	B major	♭VI	I
No. 4	'Bydlo'	G♯ minor	iv	vi
4th	'Promenade'	D minor–F major	vii–II	break
No. 5	'Chicks'	F major	II	V
No. 6	'Goldenberg'	B♭ minor	v	i
5th	'Promenade'	B♭ major	V	I
No. 7	'Limoges'	E♭ major	I	
No. 8	'Catacombs'	B minor	♭vi	
No. 9	'Baba-Yaga'	C major	VI	
No. 10	'Kiev'	E♭ major	I	

Figure 2. *Pictures at an Exhibition*: keys

orderly cycle of fifths then begins, reaching E♭ with 'Limoges'. 'Catacombs' intrusively moves to (an ambiguous) B minor. B (= C♭) minor is the submediant of E♭ minor; it gives way, in 'Baba-Yaga', to C major, the submediant of E♭ major which returns with 'Kiev'. This emphasis on the submediant keys reflects the widespread emphasis on submediant notes in the work as a whole apparent from the very first note. An important feature of key-organisation is the dual emphasis on third-relationships (which divide the octave symmetrically) and fifth-relationships (which do not). The tension between symmetry and asymmetry also appears in the harmonic organisation.

One of the most interesting features are long-range key-references. For example, G♯ (= A♭) minor is the key of several pieces, and is also referred to suddenly and unexpectedly in 'Gnomus' and 'Kiev'. 'Catacombs' makes sudden references to both C and E♭, the keys of the pieces that follow (these relationships are explored further in Chapters 6 and 7, Examples 4 and 7). Ambiguity also has a part to play. 'Catacombs' is first ambiguous between G and B then, on a larger scale, between B and F♯. F♯ is then reinterpreted as a leading note at the beginning of 'Baba-Yaga', only to find that this piece is actually in C, not G; it is not cadenced, but the final G links to the first chord of 'Kiev'.

In some senses *Pictures at an Exhibition* is a cyclic composition because of the returns and transformations of the 'Promenade' theme. Unusually, these take place outside the main fabric of the piece, in the intermezzos rather than the pictures (except in the case of 'Con mortuis' and 'Kiev'). In most appearances the 'Promenades' take the role of motto openings. *Pictures* is also sometimes regarded as a rondo or ritornello form on the basis of the recurring 'Promenades', but it is far removed from the classical conception of such forms – not least because the weight lies too much in the episodes (i.e. the pictures themselves). Fried describes this piece in terms of a combination of rondo and variation form, referring to Musorgsky as a 'master of the variation technique' on the basis that the 'Promenade' theme keeps returning in 'different psychological situations'.[5] Variation technique is important in the individual *Pictures* too. As the piece progresses, the 'Promenades' get fewer and, after 'Promenade' 5, become part of the pictures. Thus the 'Promenade' theme, which represents Musorgsky himself, shows how by the end he has been drawn into the pictures and is no longer viewing them from outside.[6]

5

Synopsis

This synopsis is a tour through Musorgsky's pieces. For each I give the basic title, include the metronome marks recalled by Stasov and Rimsky-Korsakov, discuss the underlying sketch or design, and reflect on connections with Musorgsky's other works and artistic philosophy. I also consider the formal structure. That nothing in *Pictures* remotely resembles a sonata form, the holy grail of the German 'worshippers of pure musical beauty', is not surprising given an attitude to art that puts expression before cerebration. Musorgsky's forms are highly economical, little or nothing is present as padding; once the picture has been sketched and the mood created, it is abandoned. If the forms are thought to be too abbreviated it should be remembered that, for Musorgsky, formal balance is secondary to the expression of a message. Binary and ternary forms are favoured, usually constructed in a way that minimises strong contrasts of material or tonality between sections. The principal exceptions, 'Goldenberg' and 'Catacombs'/'Con mortuis' (which must be considered a single AB structure), use strong contrast for programmatic reasons. The most clearly articulated ternary forms are 'Chicks' (the only piece that uses a 'set' instrumental form, the scherzo and trio) and 'Baba-Yaga'.

'Promenade' (French)
Allegro giusto, nel modo russico, senza allegrezza, ma poco sostenuto ($\quarternote = 104$),
B♭ major.

This is a portrait of Musorgsky, now of considerable bulk, shambling through the gallery. He remarked: 'Curious title: "Promenade" in modo russico'. Stasov explained that Musorgsky depicts 'himself there as he strolled through the exhibition; joyfully or sadly recalling the talented deceased artist', furthermore 'he does not hurry, but observes attentively'.[1]

'Promenade' is folk-inspired in its melody, its metric flexibility between 5/4 and 6/4 and its imitation of choral heterophony. There are close links between this piece and the principal idea in the coronation scene in *Boris*

Godunov (explored further in the next chapter). The 'Promenade' with its continual multi-voice chords, is devoid of pianistic figuration. Pianists should take care not to overwhelm line with harmony and need to consider adding some variety of dynamic; they may wish to introduce antiphonal effects in the central section. Although the piece should not be hurried, it is marked Allegro, and Musorgsky took great pains with his markings. Rather than a set form we move from event to event to the final cumulative statement of the theme in bar 21, barred more regularly and harmonised more normally.

(1) 'Gnomus' (Latin: Gnome)
Sempre vivo ($\quad$ = 120), E♭ minor.
Illustration lost.

We are plunged into the world of a 'fantastic lame figure on crooked little legs ... This gnome is a child's plaything, fashioned, after Hartman's design [for a nutcracker] in wood, for the Christmas tree at the Artists' Club (1869). It is something in the style of the (fabular) nutcracker, the nuts being inserted in the gnome's mouth.' In the music Stasov adds, '[the] gnome accompanies his droll movements with savage shrieks'. Frankenstein was able to identify this design as catalogue entry No. 239 in the exhibition. Both the drawing for this example of Hartman's fantastic design and the ornament itself have now disappeared.

Musorgsky turns the toy into a powerful, typically Russian, 'creative caricature', something in the manner of the grotesque little sorcerer in Glinka's *Ruslan*.[2] Fried tries to find evidence of Musorgsky's humanity here: 'Musorgsky's piece is grotesque, with a touch of tragedy, a convincing example of the humanisation of a ridiculous prototype. In the music portraying the dwarf's awkward leaps and bizarre grimaces are heard cries of suffering, moans and entreaties.'[3] She also identifies a link with the song 'Darling Savishna' (1866), where Musorgsky sets with sympathy and understanding the pleas of a village idiot in love with a local beauty.

'Gnomus' is a continuous structure whose material comprises variants and extensions of the opening figure, and of the descending idea against a rising augmented fourth that comes in bar 19. At the centre of the piece there is a sinuous chromatic melody that takes the augmented fourth as its starting point (bar 38). The opening figure makes intrusive returns throughout as the gnome stumbles. In contrast to the full harmonies of 'Promenade', much of this piece is either monodic or uses widely spaced two-part chromatic counterpoint which is inverted in the second section. This is one of the most harmonically

36

interesting pieces in the set. Diatony and functional harmonic progressions (including conventional cadential closure) are eschewed in favour of chromaticism and whole-tone influence. In the manuscript there are three cuts, two of an identical bar following bars 44 and 53 and one of an eight-bar passage after bar 53.[4]

As well as depicting the awkward gait and the frequent stumbles of the gnome, the performer must decide for himself the right balance of menace, fearfulness and sympathy for the plight of this unfortunate little character. There is an abundance of *sforzando* markings in the first part, but few other dynamics; the pianist may feel inclined to introduce a greater variety of attacks and more light and shade.

['Promenade' 2] (Musorgsky: 'intermezzo')
Moderato commodo assai e con delicatezza ($\downarrow$ = 104), A♭ major.

The second 'Promenade' provides calm and stability after 'Gnomus'. It ends on the dominant in preparation for 'Castello'. Only the first two phrases of the original are used, counterpointed by a loosely imitative voice doubled in an almost fauxbourdon-like manner. A descant soars above at the end.

(2) 'Il vecchio castello' (Italian: The Old Castle)
Andantino molto cantabile e con dolore ($\downarrow$ = 56), G♯ minor.
Illustration lost.

Stasov tells us little about the sketch beyond indicating that this is a medieval castle in front of which a troubadour is singing. There are some architectural sketches from France in the exhibition catalogue, but none from Italy.[5] Hartman added small figures to show the scale of his architectural illustrations and such is the origin of the troubadour here. This serenade with its guitar accompaniment turns into a Russian 'song without words' strongly influenced by the shapes of Russian folk music. Musorgsky's only compromise with the southern European location is the use of a siciliano rhythm. The extent to which the piece reflects Musorgsky's 'broodings on the perishable nature of our earthly existence that were tormenting him at the time' (Fried, in her notes to the facsimile autograph) is questionable.

'Castello' can be analysed as a ternary form with a second section beginning in bar 29, but the second section's melody is too like that of the first and introduction (it adopts the cadential figure of the introduction's melody in bars 35–6 and 44–5). It is probably best thought of as a song with an introduction (bars 1–7), six strophes of irregular length with freely varied materials (beginning in bars 8, 19, 29, 38, 51 and 70) and a coda which typically ends the piece with fragments of the previously heard ideas which gradually fade away.

The performer must guard against monotony in this piece; it can so easily result from the continuous G♯ pedal, the frequent tonic cadences and the generally unremarkable harmony. The melodic line, better suited to a wind instrument or voice than piano, must sing, and the siciliano rhythm must be clearly but not obtrusively present in the background. The lack of contrast between sections is a weakness; the melodies of the introduction (bars 1–7, subsequently used as a link) and the strophe beginning in bar 8, are insufficiently differentiated; that of the central section seems to grow like the earlier melodies. The coda consists of disjointed fragments of earlier material.

Less than a year after completing *Pictures*, Musorgsky employed the idea of a serenade to more powerful effect in the second song in *Songs and Dances of Death*, where death comes as a lover on a beautiful spring evening to take an invalid girl. There are strong similarities between the song and 'Castello' in melodic shapes, the siciliano rhythm and the extensive pedals above which expressive dissonant harmonies are built.

['Promenade' 3]
Moderato non tanto, pesamente, B major.

This strange dark 'Promenade' moves the key from G♯ minor to its relative, B major, preparing for 'Tuileries'; it consists largely of widely spaced two-part writing, initially weakly imitative, but giving way to a sinister left-hand chromatic scale. The whole thing peters out to octaves and unison, reflecting the endings of Russian folk songs.

(3) 'Tuileries (Dispute d'enfants après jeux)' (French: Tuileries (Dispute between Children at Play))
Allegretto non troppo, capriccioso ($\downarrow$ = 144), B major.
Illustration lost.

Stasov tells us that this little scherzo is based on a picture of children with their young nurse (plural in the first edition) playing in the Tuileries Gardens in Paris. The Hartman picture is now lost, but one is listed in the exhibition catalogue as 'Tuileries Garden, crayons'. The children were probably a detail; as we find so often, the pieces are not musical representations of Hartman's pictures, but grow out of details in them; they say more about Musorgsky than Hartman.

Musorgsky liked, and was popular with, children. Dimitri Stasov's daughter Varvara Stasova-Komarova recalled Musorgsky visiting when she was about seven years old:

he came into our child life as 'Musoryanin' as our elders called him and as we children began to call him deciding that this must be his real name ... he wasn't hypocritical with us and never talked to us in that false way that grown-up people who are friends of the family usually talk to children ... [he] always kissed our hand as if we were grown-up ladies, saying 'Good day, young lady' or 'your hand, young lady' – strange and astonishing it seemed to us, and amusing, so we came to talk with him quite freely, as with an equal.[6]

There was a certain childishness in Musorgsky's character, in a way one might almost think from his constant use of rather silly nicknames, his obsession with food and his fascination with fairy-tales, that he never quite matured. His interest in the ways of children is reflected in a number of pieces, most notably *The Nursery*. These songs reveal unprecedented understanding of how to characterise children in music without using them as an excuse for the easy and lightweight.

The atmosphere is lighter than in 'Castello': the tessitura is higher and the chords more open. The cries and taunts of the children are heard in the reiterated falling third figure. Newmarch once remarked that these are Russian, rather than French children shouting 'Nianya, Nianya' ('Nanny, Nanny'),[7] an example of Musorgsky imitating speech shapes in music. The semiquavers create a generally playful atmosphere. 'Tuileries' is best described as a rounded binary form (i.e. AB with a brief but clear return to the opening phrase at the end). Despite the double bar at bar 14, the central section, where the children adopt an attitude of mock contrition, is not strongly contrasted and we are smoothly moved back to the reworked material from the opening. As we describe in Chapter 7, some aspects of the harmonic organisation of this little piece are quite advanced.

This is one of the most pianistic pieces in the set. Ashkenazy points out that experience with orchestral versions has led pianists to take it too slowly. The metronome marking does suggest a rapid pace despite the Allegretto marking. After all 'children argue when they argue and run when they run'.[8] Great attention should be paid to the fingering; the rapid changes of full chords should still allow light, smooth performance of the quick semiquaver figuration.

(4) 'Bydlo' (Polish: Cattle)
Sempre moderato, pesante ($\text{\textquotedblright} = 88$), G♯ minor.
Illustration lost.

'Tuileries' ends lightly, playfully and quietly. Suddenly (there is no mediating 'Promenade') a huge Polish cart arrives on the scene. Musorgsky wrote to Stasov: 'Right between the eyes "Sandomirzsko bydlo" (le télégue) [the cart] it stands to reason that le télégue isn't named, but this then is between us'. But Stasov, probably aware of how Rimsky-Korsakov's replacement of Musorgsky's *fortissimo* at the opening with a crescendo destroyed the sudden entry of the cart, simply entitled the piece 'Polish cart', referring to a cart with huge wheels, pulled by oxen. By doing so he exposed Musorgsky's secret. No picture of cattle or wagon appears in the exhibition catalogue and Musorgsky's secrecy about the cart is not satisfactorily explained simply by the desire to surprise us at the opening. One might speculate that he is acknowledging some unrecorded discussion with Stasov about the scenario for this piece, or even that, given Musorgsky's Russophile tendencies, the Sandomir cattle are the Polish people themselves (on Russian attitudes to Poles and about Sandomir, see 'Goldenberg' below).

This, one of most melancholic and Russian pieces, is characterised by its thick, ponderous, left-hand chords, representing the rumbling of the wheels and the tread of hooves. It is set against a folk-like melody sung by the cart drivers which Fried tells us has Ukrainian rather than Polish characteristics. The form is ternary, without strong melodic or tonal contrast; the same accompaniment pattern continues through the central section and the coda fragments the theme. Overall length is determined by an external factor – the time it takes for the sound of the cart to die away into the distance. But, judged in purely musical terms, it is too short. The sheer weight of the musical materials needs more time to be digested.

['Promenade' 4]
Tranquillo, D minor.

This brooding 'Promenade' before the chicks begin to hatch, subjects the original material to greater change. Musorgsky, characteristically, makes no attempt to construct a modulatory interlude between the G♯ of 'Bydlo' and the F of 'Chicks'; instead he turns the music to the key of D minor. Shifting the 'Promenade' idea to the minor increases the number of melodic tritones resulting in an uneasy atmosphere added to by the sinuous, widely spaced two-part counterpoint. At the end 'Chicks' is anticipated as Musorgsky converts the dominant note of D into the mediant of F.

(5) Balet nevylupivshikhsya ptentsov
(Russian: Ballet of the Unhatched Chicks)
Scherzino vivo, leggiero ($\downarrow$ = 88), F major.
Plate 1

In the manuscript the title is pencilled in as though Musorgsky still was not content with it. In '1870 Hartman designed the costumes for the staging of the ballet *Trilbi* at the Maryinsky Theatre, St Petersburg. In the cast were a number of boy and girl pupils from the theatre school, arrayed as canaries. Others were dressed up as eggs' (Stasov to Arkady Kerzin 1903). *Trilbi* was a ballet with choreography by Marius Petipa and music by Julius Gerber (a champion of new Russian music who had performed excerpts from *Boris Godunov* in 1874). The plot was taken from the Frenchman Charles Nodier's short story 'Trilby or the Elf of Argyle' (1822). Frankenstein tracked down four of Hartman's seventeen designs for *Trilbi*. That which attracted Musorgsky was described in the exhibition catalogue as 'Canary-chicks, enclosed in eggs as in suits of armour. Instead of a head dress, canary heads, put on like helmets, down to the neck.' The designs show a side view of the complete costume, a front view with part of the helmet removed, and a side view of the helmet. No dimensions or details of materials and construction are given, but the proportions are clearly and cleverly thought out. Other designs showed Trilbi's costume to include a 'red hot poker [and] a lighted lamp in his head dress', a 'canary-notary-public' and cockatoo costumes for the men's *corps de ballet*.[9]

We have moved from the darkness of 'Bydlo' into light; from deep bass clef to high transparent writing. The peasant's toil is contrasted with the carefree world of privileged children. This is a conventional scherzino, trio and coda with largely regular four-bar phrases. The rather strange placing of the coda after the repeat of the D♭ scream is clearly specified in Musorgsky's autograph (i.e. bars 21–2 should not be cut in the reprise). The piece uses material economically. The scherzino comprises only two ideas (bars 1 and 5) and subjects them to all kinds of twists and turns as they are passed through various harmonic colours. Ostinato features in the trio. Garden finds a similar piece in Balakirev's *Humoresque* in D major (1903), but notes that he, while more pianistic is more derivative and less inventive.[10] Brown links 'Chicks' with Glinka's trio for Chernomor's march in *Ruslan*. The two pieces are scored in high registers and both begin with similar progressions alternating chords on roots F and D♭, linked by their common tone F.[11]

Effective percussive high piano sounds imitate the chicks tapping to break their shells and the little shriek as they burst out. Then difficult '*ppp*' trills (which are always whole tones starting on the upper note) depict their tiny fluffy feathers as they totter around. Birds and animals play an important part in Musorgsky's compositions. Writing to Stasov on 10/22 August 1871 (to appraise him of the text for the parrot episode in *Boris Godunov*) he gives a little catalogue of the creatures about which he has 'amiably sung'. They were to that point seven in number: a magpie, a goat, a beetle, a drake, a mosquito with a bedbug, a screech owl and a parrot. We can now add canary chicks to the list. On completing *Pictures* Musorgsky began a musical satire called 'The Hill of Nettles', in which he is depicted as a rooster who the crab (i.e. the critic and opponent of the new music Herman Laroche) accuses of screaming and shouting nonsensically and scratching in dung-heaps.

(6) '"Samuel" Goldenberg und "Schmuÿle"' (Yiddish)
Andante. Grave–energico ($\quartnote = 48$), B♭ minor.
Plates 2 and 3

With the availability of the facsimile manuscript, Musorgsky's exact Yiddish title (note the diaeresis over y and the inverted commas emphasising the Jewish names) has been revealed and a mystery cleared up. Stasov's description: 'Two Jews: rich and poor' seems to have been the source of the incorrect title being applied to many editions of this piece, including Lamm's supposedly authoritative one. Frankenstein's emphatic denial that 'Samuel Goldenberg and Schmuÿle' was the correct title led him to complex explanations involving various other lost pictures. A letter of uncertain date from Stasov to Kerzin tells us that 'Victor Hartman gave Musorgsky two of his sketches from real life, those of the rich and the poor Jew [from Sandomir]. … Musorgsky, was most delighted with the expressiveness of these pictures'.[12] Musorgsky himself probably named the two Jews.

Hartman, whose wife was Polish, visited Sandomir, a historic town in southeast Poland, on his way home from his European travels in 1868. There he painted a number of scenes and characters in the Jewish ghetto, including those for this piece and 'Bydlo'. The only other remaining picture is one of a Jewish market woman.[13] In his portrait, the rich Jew wears a comfortable fur skull cap, the symbol of his religion. The poor Jew has only a trilby, placed on top of a forlorn looking sack containing his worldly possessions. One stares out with confidence and determination as if posing, the other is captured in an attitude of hopelessness and dejection. We can hardly resist making a judgement about justice and injustice.

During the nineteenth century Poland was under Russian control, tightened after the insurrection of 1863. An atmosphere of mistrust and hatred existed between the Orthodox Russians and the Catholic and Jewish Poles. As with the unnamed little gentleman who appears during the funeral at the Marmeladov's in Dostoyevsky's *Crime and Punishment* (1866), Poles were often treated as figures of fun. More seriously, in *Boris Godunov*, the pretender plots in Sandomir, assisted by the scheming, ruthless Jesuit Rangoni (Russians despised what was for them the cerebral Catholic religion that is so much part of Polish culture). The Russian and Polish Jews, concentrated into the ghettos and refused the means of advancement, posed a considerable social problem. Many converted to Orthodox Christianity or emigrated. Others attempted to retain and emphasise their identity through their dress, religion and culture and developed the corruption of Hebrew and German that we know as Yiddish.

Despite some anti-Semitism (expected of a Russian aristocrat) in Musorgsky's letters, there is evidence of a genuine interest in Jewish culture. In 1866–7 Musorgsky lived near a Jewish family and listened to their singing. He wrote to Balakirev 'The Jews leap with joy when they hear their own songs, which are handed on from generation to generation, their eyes lighting up with honest and not pecuniary fires – I have seen this more than once'. On his tour of southern Russia in 1879 he wrote to Stasov: 'On the steamer ... to Sevastopol, ... I wrote down Greek and Jewish songs, as sung by some peasant women, and I sang the latter with them myself ... in Odessa I went to holy services in two synagogues, and was in raptures. I have clearly remembered two Israelite themes.'[14]

Several of Musorgsky's works are on Jewish texts or Old Testament themes: *King Saul* (1863), *The Destruction of Sennacherib* (1867, revised January 1874) and the *Hebrew Song* (1867). Around the time of *Pictures* he was reworking another piece with Jewish connections, the 'Song of the Libyan Warriors' (the last completed fragment the unfinished opera *Salammbô* of 1863–6), into *Jesus Navin*. This piece uses an eighteenth-century Polish Jewish melody which Musorgsky heard during the time he was living near the Jews.[15] While the similarities are not strong, some echoes of the Jewish tune can be heard in Goldenberg's melody in *Pictures*. But despite Musorgsky's interest in this music, he did not develop a distinctly Jewish or oriental style.

It is in realism, notably the portrayal of speech rhythm, that Musorgsky's true interests in 'Goldenberg' lie. Goldenberg speaks first in an assertive, blustering way with something of an oriental quality in the rhythmically intricate ornamentation and augmented intervals. He speaks slowly and clearly with a deep powerful voice, in measured lengths, pausing for breath. Then the poor Jew whines almost uncontrollably in a high voice with a triplet tremolo representing his teeth chattering or his body trembling. The B♭ minor flourishes at the end of Schmuÿle's idea have a touch of orientalism. In the end, Goldenberg, a nasty, wily and mean character, gives nothing to Schmuÿle, simply sending him off with a flea in his ear.

The AB (A+B) coda structure is determined by the underlying narrative. The sections are clearly articulated by thematic and key structure; Schmuÿle's idea is in the mediant minor. In the final section Musorgsky's desire is not to show his skill at thematic combination, but to reflect the unreconciled nature of the two protagonists. The piece is not simply a musical portrait of the two characters, but is concerned with their psychology and relationship.

Goldenberg can be played freely with an element of bluster and over-accentuation. Schmuÿle's difficult and unpianistic trembling must be played strictly. Although the tempo marking apparently changes at bar 19 the triplet idea clearly wants to proceed at the same speed, so any radical slowing here should be avoided.

['Promenade' 5]
($\downarrow$ = 104), B♭ major.

The work moves into its last phase with a restatement of the opening 'Promenade' now with extra doubling adding to its ceremonial quality.

(7) 'Limoges le marché (La grande nouvelle)' [French: The Market (The Big News)]
Allegretto vivo, sempre scherzando ($\downarrow$ = 120), E♭ major.
Illustration lost.

Stasov: 'Old women quarrelling at the fair in Limoges'. 'Hartman spent a fairly long time in the French town in 1866, executing many architectural sketches and genre pictures. The musical version of this sketch [illustrates] the crowd shrieking, disputing, chattering and quarrelling in the market place.' Hartman's drawing or painting has not come to light. It must have been one of the seventy-five from this town listed in the catalogue for the exhibition.[16]

A 'programme' in French is inserted in the autograph and then crossed out: 'La grande nouvelle: Mr de Puissangeout vient de retrouver sa vache "La Fugitive". Mais les bonnes dames de Limoges ne sont pas tout à fait d'accord sur ce sujet, parce que Mme de Remboursac s'est approprié une belle denture en porcelaine, tandis que Mr de Panta-Pantaléon garde toujours nez gênant couleur pivouane.' [The big news: Monsieur de Puissangeout has just recovered his cow 'Fugitive'. But the good wives of Limoges are not interested in this incident because Madame de Remboursac has acquired very fine porcelain dentures while Monsieur de Panta-Pantaléon is still troubled by his obtrusive nose which remains as red as a peony.]

An earlier different form of this story appears on the previous page of the manuscript where Musorgsky made a false start at the piece. There it is Monsieur Pimpant de Panta-Pantaléon whose lost cow is found and who gives contradictory answers to the trivial questions of the women about his find. The story itself is of no consequence, it is the general atmosphere that matters. Musorgsky needs to create a little scenario to make things come alive; he must imagine what people are doing and saying. Even so, realistic as the piece is, we still depend utterly on the title to understand it.

This scherzo has a ternary structure. The key signature changes at bar 12 but, as is often the case in the music of Debussy, the nature of the material and the harmonic language minimises the impact of the change. The most striking features of the piece are the calls and shouts – some comprised of whole-tone material – that interrupt its progress, and the startling foretaste of the 'Baba-Yaga' idea that intrudes before the return of the opening.[17] This is one of the most difficult pieces in the set, yet it is also the most pianistic. Like another of the French pieces, 'Tuileries', it predominantly uses the higher registers. The linking passage into 'Catacombs' is Lisztian.

(8) 'Catacombae (Sepulcrum romanum)'
Largo ($\downarrow$ = 57), B minor leads *attacca* to:
'Con mortuis in lingua mortua' (Latin: With the Dead in a Dead Language).
Andante non troppo, con lamento, B minor.
Plate 4

The coda of 'Limoges' takes us from the busy market place and casts us into the Parisian catacombs. The watercolour shows Hartman, Vasily Kenel (a friend from the Academy) and their guide, with their backs to us, examining the catacombs by lamplight. On the right is a large cage stacked full with skulls, which face us. Between 'Catacombs' and 'Con mortuis' Musorgsky has written (in Russian): 'NB: Latin text: "With the dead in a dead language"'. In the margin we also have the remark, in pencil, 'Latin text would be fine: the creative genius of the late Hartman leads me to the skulls and invokes them; the skulls begin to glow'. Musorgsky, as always, puts life into the scene, here is the very point where the composer is drawn into the pictures themselves. This idea of the skulls glowing probably came to him from the illustration where in the lamplight the skulls themselves seem to light up. Musorgsky's command of Latin was weak (there is a vocabulary mistake in the title itself: 'Con mortuis' should read 'Cum mortuis'), so he pencils his remark in the margin in Russian in the hope that it will appear translated in the printed score.

'Catacombs' and 'Con mortuis' are the most introspective pictures, reflecting the morbid side of Musorgsky at this time. Death is a recurring theme in Musorgsky's work, notably in the death of Tsar Boris. It may have deprived him of his first love, and the deaths of his mother, Hartman and Opochinina deeply affected him. Faith and religion featured little in his life, we can assume that he held little hope of an after-life. Life on earth constituted all that was available, early death was simply a waste.

The prose-like 'Catacombs', with its dissonant, unbalanced chords (notice the Stravinskian thirds in the left hand after bar 12) and uncertain tonality, is certainly not conceived in terms of piano sonority. The crescendo in bar 3 and the diminuendos on held notes over which the pianist has no control, all point to an orchestral conception. 'Con mortuis' subjects the 'Promenade' theme to an almost chant-like treatment as the skulls begin to glow. Can one hear echoes of the *Dies Irae* at the beginning? Utilising familiar material in the context of death connects this music with *Songs and Dances of Death*, where a trepak, a serenade and hymns accompany its personification. 'Con mortuis' is not an easy piece, the high tremolo must emerge from nowhere and be kept going smoothly even when the lower parts are richly doubled as the skulls reach their full illumination (bar 11).

(9) Izbushka na kur'ikh nozhkakh (Baba-Yaga)
(Russian: The Hut on Hen's Legs (Baba-Yaga))
Allegro con brio, feroce ($\s8 = 120$), C major.
Plate 5

'This piece is based on Hartman's design for a clock in the form of Baba-Yaga's hut on hen's legs, to which Musorgsky added the ride of the witch in her mortar' (Stasov in first published edition). In the exhibition catalogue: 'Baba-Yaga's hut on fowl's legs. Clock, Russian style of the fourteenth century. Bronze and enamel'. On what basis one might describe this fantastic piece of over-ornamentation as fourteenth-century is decidedly unclear.

Hartman's clock design, already partly discussed in Chapter 2, is a pencil sketch on squared paper (aiding accurate drawing of the symmetrical effects so much part of this design). The details are not fully completed.[18] The clock sits on two hen's feet (a fairy-tale motif) which stand on a plinth; it is covered in animal and bird motifs. Cocks' heads appear symmetrically out of the top and peer from one side. The clock face is surmounted by two horse's heads and there are two great gables decorated with peasant embroidery patterns. There is an abundance of rope-like and textile ornamentation. The gnarled features of the hen's legs and the unevenness of some of the plait-work offsets otherwise monotonous symmetry.

Baba-Yaga appears in Russian fairy-tales. She lives deep in the woods in a hut whose hen's legs allow it to rotate to face each unfortunate newcomer. There she lures lost children to eat them, crushing their bones in the giant mortar in which she rides through the woods propelling herself with the pestle and covering her tracks with a broomstick. Stories about witches, heroes and giants were the stuff of the fairy-tales told to Russian aristocratic children by their nurses, as Musorgsky so graphically depicts in the first song of the *Nursery* set. His only orchestral piece, *St John's Night on the Bare Mountain*, is also a setting of a supernatural tale. Less powerful settings of the Baba-Yaga legend also exist by Lyadov (a short symphonic poem) and Tchaikovsky (a piano piece).

If the metronome marking is correct, then the indication $\downarrow = 120$ leaves each bar with a duration of exactly one second; this, and the mechanical rhythm, gives the impression of a giant clock. In *Boris Godunov* the hallucinating tsar sees a vision of the child whose death placed him on the throne to the accompaniment of a ticking clock; as here hypnotic rhythm is associated with the supernatural. Musorgsky's setting, unlike Hartman's drawing, is shorn of all decoration and ornament; it is elemental and powerful while Hartman is fussy. The outer sections of the ternary structure depicting the ride of the witch are frequently monodic and equivocate between C and G. They must be played with great power. The central section mixes diminished and augmented harmonies creating tonal ambiguity and an atmosphere of spookiness not far from Bartók's 'night music'. In the manuscript, eleven bars of transition into the final section (with very similar material) have been cut.

(10) Bogatyrskie vorota (vo stol'nom gorode vo Kieve)
(Russian: The Knight's Gate (in the Ancient Capital, Kiev))
Allegro alla breve (Maestoso con grandezza) ($\mathbf{\downarrow}$ = 84), E♭ major.
Plate 6

Stasov: 'The Bogatyr's [Knight's] Gate (a gate designed by Hartman for a
competition at Kiev)' in the 'massive old Russian style, with a cupola in the
form of a Slavonic helmet'. ... 'a majestic picture in the manner of "Slavsya"
[a chorus in Glinka's *A Life for the Tsar* with strongly national connections
and melodic shapes not unlike those of Musorgsky here] and in the style of
Glinka's Ruslan Music.' 'There is a particularly lovely church motif: "As you
are baptized in Christ", and the ringing bells – are in a completely new style.'
   The competition was for a design for a grand entrance to the city of Kiev,
to commemorate Tsar Alexander II's escape from assassination by a Nihilist
there on 4 April 1866. The event encouraged the return of repression for the
remainder of Alexander's reign. The competition was called off and no gate
was built, but Hartman's design caused a stir, and he regarded it as his finest
work. The exhibition catalogue lists six views and plans. The one we know
today is described as 'Stone city-gates for Kiev, Russian style, with a small
church inside. ... The archway rests on granite pillars, three-quarters sunk
into the ground. Its head is decorated with a huge headpiece of Russian carved
designs, with the Russian state eagle above the peak. To the right is a belfry
in three stories with a cupola in the shape of a slavonic helmet.' Stasov tells
us that the tower is decorated by bricks bearing all sorts of ancient Russian
figures on the edge and corner. The Old Slavonic inscription on the arch of
the gateway reads: 'Blessed is he that cometh in the name of the Lord'. The
figure of St Michael appears on the shield on the bonnet-like wooden
headpiece (kokoshnik); kokoshnik and slavonic helmet represent female and
male. Observe too the wrought-iron work, the figures on the stained glass and
the bells that are to be so prominent in Musorgsky's setting. For Stasov,
Hartman's design passed muster because it had two essential qualities: ancient
Russianness and originality. It gave the impression of the 'old heroic Russia'.
The columns, he wrote, 'seem sunk into the earth as though weighted down
with old age, and as though God knows how many centuries ago they had been
built. Above, instead of a cupola is a Slavonic war helmet with pointed peak.
The walls are decorated with a pattern of coloured brick! How original is
this!'[19] The idea of a column half sunk into the ground had occurred to
Hartman before, he had used it as a student in designing a monument to an
architect; the design won him a prize.

Kiev was the birthplace of Christianity in Russia where in AD 988 Vladimir of Kiev became Christian and ordered a mass baptism of his people in the Dnieper. The roots of ancient Russian church music lie in the links between Kiev and Byzantium. Musorgsky's piece includes a reworking of the Russian hymn identified by Stasov above, but his setting does not reveal a very deep understanding of what ancient Russian Church music was like (see Chapter 6). This hymn has nothing to do with Musorgsky's faith, or lack of it, it is there because of associations with Russian history and culture and because of the chapel in Hartman's design.

Musorgsky's piece matches the grandness of Hartman's concept. 'Kiev' is a collage of hymn and bell sounds which moves to a mighty climax only fully attainable in the orchestra. The key is E♭, the pitch associated in *Boris* with the 'impending death of the tsar'[20] (a deathly reference to this key already occurred towards the end of 'Catacombs'). The opening processional melody must be played with power, but something should be left in reserve for the final pages. The first forty-six bars are remarkable for their completely unadorned chordal writing and lack of pianistic figuration. Musorgsky's method of construction is typically Russian. The opening processional tune is presented in three guises, first plainly, then adorned with pealing bells and finally it is given a climactic triplet rhythm. In between we get the stark statements of 'As you are baptised in Christ' (marked *senza espressione*) and one massive interlude of Russian bell sounds (bars 81–112) which incorporates the return of the opening 'Promenade' theme. The bell sounds form a pulsating, dissonant mass (each layer of which should be played equally). Bell sounds are employed elsewhere in Musorgsky, notably in *Boris Godunov*.[21] Pedals are very much part of this piece and no more so than in the final coda for which the greatest weight should be reserved. In 1875, perhaps influenced by 'Kiev', Stasov suggested the death of a fanatical monk in his cell to the accompaniment of distant bells as a scenario for a song to Musorgsky and Kutuzov; they did not take up the idea. The influence of this piece is widespread, and can be strongly felt in Borodin's 'Au Couvent' (1885) and Debussy's 'La Cathédrale engloutie' (1910).

Plate 1 V. Hartman. Canary Chicks in their Shells; a costume sketch for
Gerber's ballet *Trilbi*. Watercolour; 17.6×25.3 cm.

Plate 2 V. Hartman. A Rich Jew in a Fur Hat.
Pencil, sepia, lacquer; 25.6×19.9 cm.

Plate 3 V. Hartman. A Poor Jew. Pencil, watercolour; 14×10.5 cm.

Plate 4 V. Hartman. Paris Catacombs (including Hartman, V. Kenel and guide with lantern). Watercolour; 12.9×17cm.

Plate 5 V. Hartman. Baba–Yaga's Hut on Hen's Legs. Sketch for a clock in Russian style. Pencil; 23.5×31.8 cm.

Plate 6 V. Hartman. Design for Kiev City Gate: Main Façade.
Pencil, watercolour; 42.9×60.8 cm.

6

The musical language of
'Pictures at an Exhibition'

Folk music

Pictures divides into the obviously folk-inspired pieces with diatonic, conjunct melody and a simpler harmonic style ('Promenade', 'Castello', 'Bydlo' and 'Kiev') and the more instrumental ones with chromatic melody and more advanced harmonic techniques where the influence of folk music is less overt ('Gnomus', 'Tuileries', 'Chicks' and 'Limoges'). Musorgsky is essentially a linear composer and the shapes of Russian folk music are often detected in his melodies, but they also affect his harmonic language. He was never a systematic folk-song collector but he listened to native folk singing as a child in the Russian countryside and he always had an ear for national songs and folk singers such as Trofim Ryabinin (a song of whose was employed in *Boris*). Furthermore, he was particularly keen, when composing *Khovanshchina* during the 1870s, to seek out authentic melodies of the Old Believers. Balakirev's collecting and arranging of folk music and his use of the material to transform his own musical language also had a profound effect upon Musorgsky. Actual folk melodies are not employed in *Pictures* (with the exception of the chorale melody loosely used in 'Kiev'), but folk-influence may be felt in a variety of ways, most significantly in modal alterations, a narrow range, obsessively reiterated small diatonic collections, heterophony, parallelism and the use of pedals.

Russian folk music, which favours the major or natural minor modes, is often modally wayward (*peremennost*), shifting from one tonic to another. Melodies may be found to have a tonic a tone lower at the end of a song or phrase (as in Musorgsky's 'study in folk style' 'Kalistratushka' (1864) where the vocal melody begins in F♯ minor but cadences on E four bars later). A little of this quality can be found in the opening 'Promenade' whose shifts through various harmonic regions (see p. 57) may owe more to *peremennost* than to conventional harmonic processes. Perhaps surprisingly for the Western reader, the pentatony at the opening of the piece is not common in Russian folk music,

50

and this is its most striking appearance in Musorgsky's output.

The tonal flavour of Russian folk music tends to come from alterations made to the two basic modes. Alterations such as flattened sixths and supertonics and sharpened fourths all occur in *Pictures*. These affect the major or minor modality of triads, the nature of cadences, the raising and lowering of the leading note and so on. In Musorgsky this kind of process leads to what may be termed a variable scale (i.e. a scale including both raised and diatonic sixth and seventh degrees and the raised and diatonic fourth). Vacillations such as that between the major and minor thirds, E♭ and E♮, (B♭ ii/II) in the opening 'Promenade' are the result of variable scale writing. Alterations made to the diatonic scales can often bring them into contact with other more exotic ones such as the interpenetration of diatonic and whole-tone modes in 'Gnomus' (see Chapter 7).

'Castello' is the most modal piece in the set. Its principal melody is Aeolian, the natural seventh degree is much in evidence, but the raised seventh does tend to appear in the inner parts particularly at cadences (in this sense Musorgsky's folk style in *Pictures* is less pure than in some of his songs or Balakirev's folk settings which tend to eschew the raised leading note altogether). The third strain emphasises the characteristic minor sixth degree (E), the flattened supertonic (A) and the raised fourth (C$^{\times}$ = D) and triads built upon these degrees, creating richly expressive dissonance with the underlying G♯ pedal. This means of raising expressiveness at the centre of pieces or sections is also used in 'Kiev' and *Sunless*.

Raised and lowered leading notes and fourths produce the striking orientalism at the beginning of 'Goldenberg'. In the context of B♭ Musorgsky incorporates two augmented seconds D♭/E and G♭/A. (Notice too the diminished fourth A/D♭ in bars 7–8.) In 'Baba-Yaga' there is the constant modal mixing of C minor and C major, the strong presence of the flattened sixth (A♭), the lowered seventh (B♭), and the raised fourth F♯, the latter being substantially responsible for the ambiguity between C and G. The rarity of dominant–tonic progressions in either key, and a general absence for much of the time of the leading note (B) further contributes to the ambiguity. The resultant lack of harmonic thrust necessitates the employment of powerful motor rhythms.

'Castello' contains some diatonic melismatic writing, which may reflect the influence of a type of melismatic peasant song known as the *protyazhnaya*.[1] This type of song has a tendency for the opening statement to ornament a fifth falling to the tonic, a characteristic found at the beginning of 'Castello' and a number of other pictures. 'Bydlo' shows the same influence and is in the

51

Example 1. Similar melodic shapes in 'Promenade', *Boris Godunov*
and Russian folk songs

(a) 'Promenade'

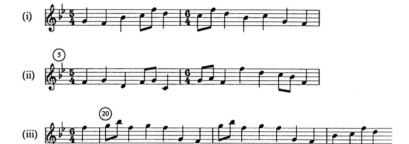

(b) *Boris Godunov*, Prologue to Scene 2

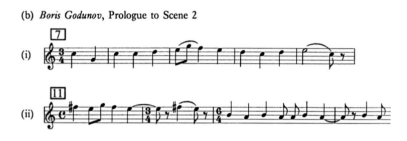

(c) Folk songs

same key, G♯ minor. Here the end of the falling fifth is placed an octave higher
(play or sing the final five notes of the opening phrase an octave lower and
its association with the *protyazhnaya* becomes clearer). In the second section
(bars 21–37) the melody alone suggests tonicising F♮, the natural minor leading
note – a quality closely associated with the folk model; but Musorgsky's richly
inventive harmony tonicises ♭II instead and F♮ is harmonised as the third of

A:IV. This tonicisation of the flat supertonic follows on from the use of that chord in bar 5 to articulate the second phrase, reflecting a tendency of Russian folk music to make an early emphasis on the second degree of the scale.

Out of context the opening melody in 'Bydlo' could be heard as Phrygian (a rare mode in Russian folk music) on D♯, with the characteristic flattened second, E. Although this is ultimately a mistaken interpretation, it is significant that the Phrygian qualities of the chorale beginning in bar 30 of 'Kiev' are dealt with in the same way, and that chorale is in the enharmonically equivalent key of A♭ minor. The fading out to a single note in 'Bydlo' reflects Russian folk music. But in general the plagal cadences and melodic cadential formulas of Russian folk music are not much in evidence in *Pictures*; one exception is the archaic v–vi–i ending to the chorale in 'Kiev' (bars 43–5).

As mentioned in the previous chapter, there are melodic similarities between the 'Promenade' theme (Example 1a) and the 'Slava' melody (the Russian hymn 'Glory to God in the Highest') used in the coronation scene in *Boris* (Example 1b).[2] On examining Examples 1a and 1b we find that both reiterate, in typical Russian fashion, motifs based on rising and falling diatonic seconds and fourths and the distinctive ♪♪♩ rhythm, in changing metric contexts. Example 1c gives two other Russian tunes identified in Lvov and Prác's collection by Hübsch;[3] they both begin similarly to the 'Promenade' idea (but neither is pentatonic). Not every melody in *Pictures* is as close to Russian folk song as that of 'Promenade', but the tendency to reiterate distinctive rhythmic and melodic shapes established at the outset of each piece is frequently in evidence.

Heterophony is also a common feature of 'Promenade' and the coronation scene. In heterophony, 'starting with a solo intonation (*zapevalo*), the ensemble of singers would without any warning split into parts, each of which was also a self-sufficient melody not too divergent from the one that could conceivably be termed "principal"'.[4] Musorgsky was the first composer to 'attempt to re-create Russian folk heterophony in all of its details',[5] and its influence can be heard in some of his choral music. As Morosan points out, his use of this style came in advance of the first collection of folk music that attempted to present Russian folk tunes 'in their original state of choral heterophony', which did not come until 1879. Swan reproduces the wedding song 'Da svaty moi' ('So, my marriage brokers'), from Listopadov's collection (see Example 2), which has close parallels with 'Promenade'.[6] The song begins with a diatonic solo in the tenor (notated in 6/4 by the collector) with the stronger first and third beats marked by pairs of quavers. With typical modal waywardness the melody, initially Dorian on G, wanders through D minor

Example 2. 'Da svaty moi': a Russian heterophonic folk song from
Listopadov's collection (after Swan)

to B♭. The accompanying voices follow the rhythm of the tune almost exactly.
The tenor is a variant of the soprano, the alto has a similar relationship with
the bass. The bass line is strong with frequent contrary motion, just as in
'Promenade'.

The harmonic style that results from heterophony will be governed by linear
considerations to a greater extent than in a chorale which has a superficially
similar harmonic rhythm. Musorgsky's progressions, while hardly non-
functional, are largely concerned with pointing-up the wayward modality of
the tune. They reflect the folk characteristic of holding notes between chords
and utilising inner pedals. The number of parts increases and decreases at will
and we notice the folk-derived gravitation to G and F becoming more
prominent as the music progresses. Folk-like too are the bare fifths and
octaves. Parallel fifths appear as early as the third and fourth chord; this result
of trying to re-create the rough-hewn sonority of folk heterophony should not
be seen as a weakness in Musorgsky's musical grammar. Parallels are
prominent elsewhere in *Pictures*, not least at the beginning of 'Tuileries' and
in bars 5–8 of 'Chicks' – in both cases Musorgsky is seeking new kinds of

Example 3. The Russian Orthodox hymn 'As you are baptised
in Christ' (after Hübsch)

sonority. Mixing parallelism and varying degrees of harmonic function is very much part of his style and looks forward to the music of his successors, notably Debussy.

Church music and bell sounds

The hymn and the bell sounds in 'Kiev' link us to music of the Russian Church. Musorgsky did not write any church music but its influence appears in his secular works when he wishes to portray clerical characters and, in this case, a chapel. It is tempting to think of Musorgsky as being influenced by the ancient Russian *Znamenny* chant which originated in Byzantium and took on many characteristics of folk music. But as Russian culture looked towards the West in the eighteenth century the chant was submerged and only official Westernised church music was permitted. It seems likely that Musorgsky only had a slight acquaintance with traditional Russian church music, despite his claim that at the Guards' school, he 'sedulously sought the company of the religious instructor, Father Krupsky, and thanks to him succeeded in penetrating deep into the very essence of old church music, Greek and Catholic'.[7] As Morosan states there 'is no documentary evidence that Musorgsky recognised the ancient chant traditions as being an indispensable aspect of Russia's musical heritage which, along with the folk song, might have served him as a rich source of musical ideas'.[8] It appears that Musorgsky, who sang in the school choir, showed interest in the music performed there and Krupsky had consequently shown him works by Bortniansky (1751–1825) and other more recent composers.[9]

When he came to write the hymn at bar 30 in 'Kiev', Musorgsky imitated the simpler derivatives of the old chants shorn of their characteristic

55

melismatic features – and set in a harmonic style more reminiscent of Lutheran chorale than true Russian Orthodox church music – found in the 'Obikhod' (the official collection of church music disseminated by the Imperial chapel during the nineteenth century). The original hymn 'As you are baptised in Christ' is given in Example 3.[10] Musorgsky increases its range, but removes what few melismatic features it had. The original tune is Phrygian, but his harmonisation in A♭ minimises this quality. Progressions such as F♭ vi–V–I– V (bars 32–4) are directly comparable with those of nineteenth-century harmonisations of Kievan and Greek chants identified by Morosan,[11] as is the tendency for chords to group in threes, each group beginning and ending with the same one (perhaps in a different inversion).

The Phrygian mode was uncommon in Russian church music but Morosan points to passages in *Boris Godunov* and *Khovanshchina* where Musorgsky similarly invoked it in religious contexts. The 'Kiev' chorale, while still a long way from ancient Russian church music, has rather more plagalism and modalism than Glinka's 'Slavsya' praised by Stasov in his letter quoted in Chapter 2. Elsewhere he refers to 'Slavsya' as a melody composed 'entirely in the character of our ancient Russian and Greek church melodies, harmonized with the plagal cadence of the Middle Ages'.[12] In practice Stasov and his friends knew little of ancient Russian church music, let alone music of the Middle Ages.

As the hymn comes to an end for the second time in bar 81 interesting bell sounds are heard. Russian bell ringing is not the same as English change-ringing where a single line emerges as the result of the ringers sounding their bells in sequence. In Russian ringing, layers of bell sounds are superimposed on one another such that the high bells sound rapidly and the deeper ones more slowly, each layer containing a repeated diad. Russian bells do not swing, but are hit by hammers, so precisely synchronised layers are possible. The harmonies produced are often dissonant and, because bells were often constructed at different times, out of tune. Musorgsky begins with sustained minims and semibreves representing the deeper bells. More rapid, less sustained layers are then added above, first in triplet crotchets, then in quavers. The chords produced alternate between E♭ II$^7_5$ and ♭II^7; the lower notes are widely spaced but the higher ones are closer together, creating bell-like clashes. Despite the difficulties in transcribing the bell texture for piano, it is generally possible to identify each voice's recurring note or diad. The most striking portrayal of Russian bells is at the beginning of the coronation scene of *Boris Godunov*. There the resources of the orchestra allow more, and more sharply defined, layers to be created and the harmonic language, based on the octatonic juxtaposition of two dominant sevenths with roots a tritone apart, is rather more striking and original than in 'Kiev'. In our piece, II and ♭II prepare the dominant which emerges as a bass pedal in bar 93 above which (bars 97–102) the bells ring out the 'Promenade' theme. The dominant pedal descends to the tonic prematurely in bar 107 above which the upper layers of bells ring out a dissonant pentatonic V^7_4 chord (which should resolve to V^7_3 but fails to do so). The tonic is finally, climactically, achieved in bar 114.

The variation process

Musorgsky is very economical in his use of material. Each piece seems to be generated by a process of continual melodic variation, owing much to the reiteration and reworking of tiny cells in Russian folk music and little to Germanic developing variation. The development of short figures or motifs in a highly logical, abstract tonal environment ('musical mathematics' as Musorgsky called it) had no appeal for the progressive Russians. Most pieces contain disruptions and discontinuities which form an important part of the variation process.

Musorgsky's treatment of the 'Promenade' theme provides a straightforward example of his technique. The melody grows out of the motifs described above by processes such as permutation, inversion and transposition. Each phrase evolves out of its predecessor until, at the end of bar 21, we receive a restatement of the opening theme. The larger course of the piece is influenced by its wayward modality. It ends in B♭ but this is by no means certain at the opening where the tonality could equally well be G Aeolian or F major. In the first half, disruption and discontinuity are, typically, important to the rhetoric of the piece. In bar 8, the end of a repeated phrase is abruptly transposed up a minor third while the key falls by a major third from F to D♭. In bar 12, the music of bar 9, which has appeared minus its final beat as bar 11, is suddenly transposed up a major third to F major. This leaves the D♭: V^4_2 (the essential harmony in bar 11) irregularly resolved. From bar 16 disruption is replaced by ambiguity as the key of B♭ attempts to assert itself over F. The final stage in the variation process is the presentation of the theme in B♭ major and 6/4 metre clarifying earlier ambiguities.

This process is shaped by the phrase-structure. The piece begins with regular two-bar phrases, pairing neatly into four-bar periods until bar 12 where the pattern is broken by the absence of the expected repeat of bar 10 and the intrusive return to F major. In the second half the phrases are less regular and tend to run into one another; there is also the gradual incursion of the unison interjections. A broad characteristic of *Pictures* is its tendency for pieces to begin with regular structures with short phrases and move towards complexity and fragmentation.

In 'Gnomus' too the piece evolves by repeating, varying and adding to the basic ideas (bars 1–2 and the bass idea beginning with a rising tritone, bars 19–20). In the ternary structure spanning bars 1–37, the first section is constructed by attaching two distinct endings to the bar 1 idea and the central section by counterpointing the rising bass with descending chords. Phrases in the first part are three bars long but have intrusive, single-bar, *sforzando* B♭ unisons. In the central section, they are four bars long; B♭ again intrudes at the end. From bar 27 the intrusive B♭'s have C♭ neighbours attached, making an explicit motivic connection with the opening.

The remainder of the music divides in two (bars 38–71 and bar 72 to the end). First, the opening tritone from bars 20–1 is the catalyst for a sinuous melody which begins in unison and then breaks into two parts continually disrupted by intrusive returns of the opening idea (notably in A♭ minor in bar 54). We notice the melody-building technique, also used in 'Promenade', of beginning a repeat but then suddenly transposing half way through – compare bars 40 and 49. The tessitura becomes higher as the tension increases, reaching its high point in bar 60. From bar 72 there is a variation on bars 19–26 characterised by the trills and bass runs. After two ferocious outbursts in A♭ minor the piece ends with a rapid coda. The A♭ minor chords feature a 5–6♭ motion in the upper voice; the coda begins with 6♭–5 in E♭ (C♭–B♭). The interesting harmonic and scalar qualities and their relationship to the overall structure of this piece will be discussed in Chapter 7. It is sufficient to note here that the piece is anchored to E♭ simply by its frequent use as a prominent bass note and pedal. Modulation and change of key play little part in articulating the formal structure which is simply a sequence of events.

In 'Castello' the various strophes are all broadly similar; in each the same melodic ideas seem to take slightly different courses. The Musorgskian device of beginning as though repeating exactly, but then diverting quite suddenly creating a small point of disruption, is well used here (see bar 21). The same procedure may be found in 'Tuileries'. For example, in bar 8 the regular pattern of repeated two-bar phrases is broken by an unexpected harmony and a reworking of the previous bar's motif rather than the one anticipated; the two-bar phrases are suddenly reduced to only one bar. Similar techniques feature in 'Limoges' which also illustrates the tendency towards fragmentation in the final stages of a piece or section (bars 33–6).

The 'Promenades', together with 'Con mortuis' and the climactic treatment of the theme in 'Kiev', provide the most obvious examples of thematic transformation in *Pictures*. The treatment of the theme is Russian in that it sets the same idea, without radical change, in a variety of colours and contexts. The second 'Promenade' utilises only the first two phrases of the original and is tonally less ambiguous. The tune is placed in the tenor, with right-hand chords soaring above, freely imitating the shapes of the tenor's line with typical infelicities of voice-leading. Towards the end the tune is doubled fauxbourdon-like (not a Russian folk characteristic) in the right hand against falling fifths in the left. In the final two bars a 'soprano' soars above reminding us that 'in Russian folk choirs: sopranos are rare, only one or two to the group, and they harmonise above the central line of melody, providing the pedal effects above'.[13]

The tiny 'Promenade' 3 utilises two-part writing. It would have been easy to have begun the bass line in exact imitation of the right hand; but such strictness of contrapuntal technique has no place in Musorgsky for it tends to draw attention to itself as a technique. 'Promenade' 4 removes the first two notes from the theme but from then on transposes it up a third from B♭ major to D minor introducing augmented fourths in the melody. In 'Con mortuis' the 'Promenade' theme is varied more. Only the first eight bars of the 'Promenade' are used. Although the idea again begins on G, its placing in B minor has a significant effect upon the interval structure removing any suggestion of pentatony; the tonal ambiguity is now between B and F♯ minors. The various 'Promenades' not only change the key colour and vary the melody slightly, they also alter its scalar character and introduce new ambiguities.

Pictures is not only unified by the transformations of the 'Promenade' theme, but also by recurrences of basic scale steps 6–5 and 1–2–3 derived from it. These two motifs, together with another 5–4♯ figure, are summarised in Example 4; they may be traced through all the principal thematic ideas and complement the links forged through key-structure explained in Chapter 4. Fixed pitch relationships are important as well as the motifs themselves. A very important series is that connected with the pitches F♭/E and E♭/D♯ in the keys of A♭ minor and G♯ minor. G♯ is the key of two pieces ('Castello' and 'Bydlo') which are strongly related in their thematic shapes. A♭ is the key of the second 'Promenade', but is more significantly the key of the interruption in 'Gnomus' (bar 54) which prepares us for a set of fixed pitch relationships extending to the chorale in 'Kiev'. Numerous other links are discernible from the example such as the way the final G♯ at the end of 'Castello' becomes the first note of the third 'Promenade', or the way C–B♭ at the end of 'Promenade' 5 becomes C♭–B♭ in 'Limoges'. Some further backward and forward fixed-

59

Example 4. Motifs 1–2–3, 6–5 and 5–4♯

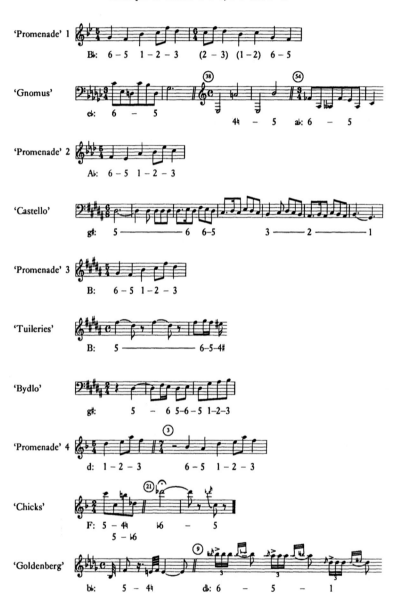

Example 4 (*cont.*). Motifs 1–2–3, 6–5 and 5–4♮

pitch references in 'Catacombs' not shown in Example 4 will be discussed in Chapter 7. The principal theme in 'Kiev' not only derives from the 1–2–3 motif, but also confirms the prominence of G, the opening note of the work; closure is finally effected when this third is taken down to the tonic at the end (see Example 7 in chapter 7). One striking feature of 'Kiev' is the way the principal motif (6–5) becomes ♭6–5–1 in the bass throughout the bell passage (bars 81–113) powerfully directing the music towards its climax.

Rhythm and metre

'Promenade' is often cited as an example of Musorgsky's 'Russian' metric fluidity; but it is not a general quality of this work in which most pieces use only one metre. The effectiveness of the 'Promenades' partly arises from their flexibility contrasting with regular metres in the pieces around them. The rhythmic patterns are usually uncomplicated; only in 'Goldenberg' do we find a degree of intricacy. Each piece tends to have its own distinctive rhythmic pattern. Given that harmonic suspensions are not a feature of Musorgsky's writing, it is not surprising that syncopation appears rarely; the trio of 'Chicks', literally the most four-square piece in terms of phrase structure, is the only example of its consistent use. Some syncopation does appear in 'Gnomus', which also features off-beat *sforzando* accents, rhythmic disruptions and hemiola-like effects; true hemiola occurs at the end of 'Kiev'. 'Limoges' also has frequent off-beat *sforzando* accents (five in bar 3 alone).

There is some rhythmic interest in this piece at the level of phrase length. Musorgsky's juxtaposition of 5/4 and 6/4 makes an eleven-beat unit at the beginning of the work, reflecting his liking for prime numbers. If we count bars or crotchets as appropriate we will find some unconventional phrases and strophes elsewhere. The strophes of 'Castello' are all of irregular lengths; in the centre of 'Gnomus' we find seven-bar phrases (bars 38–45 and 47–53); in the centre of 'Bydlo' eleven-bar units (bars 10–20 and 27–37). 'Con mortuis' falls into two halves, each with sixty crotchets (plus the first section is prefaced by three upbeats) with an irregular first section (3+1, 12, 15, 15, 17) contrasting with a regular second (4×12). In 'Baba-Yaga' the regular outer sections contrast with the inner one where asymmetrically divided fourteen-crotchet (8+6) units are characteristic (bars 96–9, 100–103, 104–7, 108–11, 112–15); the final section, bars 116–22, contains twenty-eight (2×14) crotchets.

Harmony, scales, tonality and voice-leading in 'Pictures at an Exhibition'

Harmonic techniques in *Pictures* are many and varied. Just as each picture has its own formal structure, so each has its own characteristic harmonic procedures. Musorgsky's vocabulary of chords is unremarkable except for a few whole-tone and octatonic products; it is the way they are employed that is original and varied. Superficially, Musorgsky's harmony often adds colour and weight to an essentially linear structure, rather than having a structural function itself. But deeper consideration does reveal great sensitivity to long-range harmonic structuring.[1] Musorgsky was able to judge by ear the harmonic weight and potential of chords in many situations, relating them in ways that are only now becoming clear. His restrained use of passing and auxiliary notes and the almost complete absence of suspensions are symptomatic of a technique in which each vertical has harmonic potential. This makes a reductional approach of the Schenkerian kind difficult in the more advanced pieces, inclining us to more radical methods such as pitch-class set analysis and to the study of new scales and aggregates and of new modes of linear analysis. There is little or no imitative counterpoint; while the kind of free polyphony that derives from folk heterophony and free two-part writing are widespread, strict imitative counterpoint and any kind of quasi-fugal writing have no place in Musorgsky.

Indeed, in many ways Musorgsky's methods look beyond the theory of his time. He had little respect for the conventions of musical grammar, being more interested in sonorities than rules. The castigation of much of Musorgsky's music for its lack of sound harmonic technique is one of the great injustices perpetrated upon him by his contemporaries. It is true that Musorgsky lacked polish in handling one particular type of compositional technique: the sophisticated major-minor tonal system of the nineteenth-century German composers with its complex prolongational procedures and highly complex functional harmony (but compensating lack of sophistication in melodic procedures and rhythm), often encapsulated in a sonata form. But this type of abstract tonal sophistication is of little relevance to Musorgsky's structures; indeed, it may well detract from what he is expressing.

Had Musorgsky lived longer 'the history of tonality in the late nineteenth century and the transition to atonality in the early twentieth would have assumed an entirely different chronological profile'.[2] Such words only make sense if we recognise that far from revealing deficiencies, some of the stranger harmonic and other structural aspects of this music arise from the introduction of, for their time, far-sighted procedures such as whole-tone and octatonic writing and the creation of pitch-class priority through means other than functional progression. Indeed, 'normal' functional writing is but one colour in a rich palette; we should not criticise Musorgsky for its quality, but look to the effect produced when it is mixed with a rich variety of other shades, whether blended or starkly juxtaposed.

As we noted earlier, in some of Musorgsky's poorer piano music the influence of Balakirev's harmony is strong, but it appears rarely in *Pictures*; we may detect a hint of his teacher in the most oriental piece, 'Goldenberg', with the progression B♭ minor III–III$^{5♯}$ ... I (bars 25–6) with its raised fifth in the second chord. Balakirev's incessant modulation is not found in *Pictures*. Within individual pieces substantive modulations are rare and changes of key tend not to be anticipated or prepared; they take place when the moment demands. Key signatures of more than three flats or sharps are common, particularly in the earlier part of the work; a few years later a fervent admirer, Claude Debussy, was to show a similar interest in more exotic signatures.

The widespread use of diminished sevenths and the extension of mediant relationships is a feature of nineteenth-century music and particularly of Russian music from Glinka onwards. In 'Goldenberg' the second section is in the mediant minor with a melodic emphasis on the submediant note (B♮) as part of a ♭6–5 motion in that key. Seventh chords of all kinds are widespread in *Pictures*; they are used in unconventional ways and sometimes as free-standing sonorities without an obligation to resolve, reflecting a free and expressive attitude to dissonance most apparent in 'Catacombs'. The flat-submediant chord, often with seventh attached or recast as a German sixth, is a particular favourite, reflecting a desire to move from functional dominant–tonic harmony to a more colourful palette (dominant–tonic progressions may be absent for considerable periods in this work). A good example comes at the beginning of 'Chicks' where a German sixth prolongs the tonic without progressing through the dominant. On a larger scale there is the more extended reference to G major in bars 20–1 of the B major 'Tuileries'.

Sets and scales

In 'Gnomus', the forward-looking scalar and harmonic procedures contrast with the more conventional ones in the pieces around it. Functional harmony plays little part in the establishment of Eb minor. Tonic triads appear rarely, dominant triads are completely absent; but contextual emphasis is placed on the tonic and dominant notes, particularly in the bass; there are no conventional cadences. Each section seems to be concerned with its own particular type of harmonic process, both to characterise the section itself and to differentiate it from its neighbours, something quite progressive in 1874.

The goal of the first seventeen entirely monodic bars is clear: they gravitate to the dominant note, Bb, which falls to the tonic in the bass of bar 19 (as in Debussy, though there may be scalar and harmonic complexities, the bass ensures a clear sense of harmonic direction). As with 'Promenade', the piece begins on the sixth degree of the scale, falling to the fifth on the third beat. This, plus the leading note Dᵇ suggests Eb minor despite the strong contextual emphasis on Gb in bar 2. The opening eighteen bars employ a seven-note collection with an interpenetration of Eb minor, Phrygian, chromatic and whole-tone qualities. The supertonic is flattened (Phrygian), the fourth, Ab, is missing (preventing the formation of the tritone Ab/D which could help reinforce the Eb tonality) and, in bars 5–10 and 12–17, a descending whole-tone tetrachord (Gb, Fb, D, Bb) is outlined: see Example 5a.

The pitch material of this monodic opening section contrasts with that in the next (bars 19–28) with its non-functional progression which makes use of appoggiaturas (rare in this work) on the downbeats. The distinctive raised leading note and Phrygian lowered second of the previous section have now been removed, but the tritone, A, and the raised sixth, C, are added to the Eb minor collection, giving it a quite different quality. The progression is held together by the constant presence of Eb and Gb and is built on the fact that the diminished and minor triads on the tonic are differentiated by A and Bb (a distinctive feature of Russian nineteenth-century harmony is the connection of chords through common tones rather than functional relationships). This progression crystallises in bar 38 into an important trichord – Eb, Aᵇ, Bb, 3–5: [3, 9, 10] in Forte's nomenclature – which is then extensively exploited in the distinctive writing of the next section beginning in bar 38.[3]

In the form just given, 3–5 contains the tonic and its diatonic fifth and diminished fifth (= augmented fourth). In the melody of bars 38–44 it is followed by semitonal, almost cluster-like, material. This combination is

Example 5. Sets and scales in 'Gnomus'

(a)

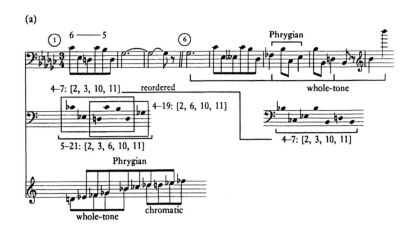

(b)

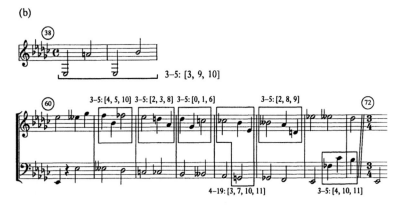

turned, in bars 60–71, into an extraordinary prolongation of E♭ using invertible counterpoint presenting 3–5s in a great variety of permutations and transpositions, and chromatic material (which also characterises this section) simultaneously. First the right hand takes the succession of 3–5s as the left hand descends chromatically, then the roles are reversed. E♭'s at each end ensure tonal coherence without resorting to functional harmony (see Example 5b).

The use of pitch-class set nomenclature here is appropriate because 3–5 is subject to so many reorderings and transpositions; it is being manipulated in a way that looks forward to the post-tonal music of a quarter of a century later. Pitch-class set nomenclature also serves to distinguish the materials here from those in previous sections. For example, beneath Example 5a are shown the sets formed by the important opening figure in 'Gnomus': 4–7: [2, 3, 10, 11] (subsequently reordered to conclude each nine-bar section) and 4–19: [2, 6, 10, 11], both subsets of 5–21: [2, 3, 6, 10, 11]. Set 3–5 is not a subset of any of these, nor are any of the chromatic sets with more than two pitch classes. The significance of this is increased when we realise that these sets all occur widely in post-tonal music composed in the final years of the nineteenth and early years of the twentieth centuries. Musorgsky can be seen to be looking forward to the sonorities of pieces such as Schoenberg's Piano Piece Op. 11 no. 1 where 4–19 is frequently found embedded in 5–21 and the piece ends with a chord (4–9) which contains three forms of 3–5. The set 4–7 is also popular with post-tonal composers partly because of its symmetrical qualities (the juxtaposition of 4–19 and 4–7 plays a significant role in the harmonic organisation of Webern's Bagatelle Op. 9 no. 1 for string quartet).[4]

Furthermore, these sets are common elsewhere in Musorgsky's output. For example, 4–19 is widespread in various permutations, transpositions and inversions in the music of *Boris Godunov*. When near the end of 'Gnomus' we have a sudden move to the subdominant minor (referring back to bars 54–7) with the interjection of the chords at 'sempre vivo', the dissonant F♭ added to the subdominant chord is unresolved and produces another frequently occurring set in Musorgsky: 4–20: [3, 4, 8, 11], a sonority which Forte points out in Musorgsky's work is without need of resolution. In *Boris* it becomes, in various permutations and transpositions, the Dimitri motif.[5] Finally, 5–21, 4–7, 4–19 and 3–5 are all subsets of 6–Z19 (another frequently occurring set in the post-tonal repertoire) which plays a significant role in 'Tuileries'.

The octatonic scale had particular appeal for Russian composers beginning with Rimsky-Korsakov's *Sadko* of 1867.[6] In Musorgsky, the repeated juxtaposition of two dominant sevenths on roots a tritone apart to form the bell chords in the coronation scene in *Boris* is a distinctive octatonic progression. The somewhat novel harmonic language of 'Tuileries' seems in places to arise from the mixing of octatonic and diatonic writing, though the complex interpenetration of the two does seem to suggest that there is octatonic flavouring here rather than overt systematic use of the scale. As shown in Example 6a, the melodic and harmonic content of bars 1–4 comprises a hexachord drawn from an octatonic scale on B: B, B♯, C×, D♯, E♯, F♯, G♯. Since

Example 6. Octatony, diatony and set 6–Z19 in 'Tuileries'

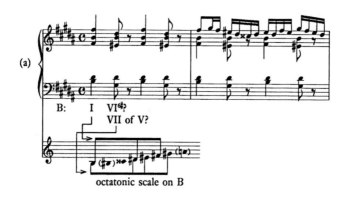

octatonic scale on B

F♯ major

6–Z19: [2, 3, 5, 6, 10, 11]

the octatonic scale is a symmetrical sequence of whole and half steps the desired tonic must be imposed contextually. Here B is constantly reiterated both in the bass and as an inner voice until bar 8 and the piece opens with a B major triad. The second chord with qualities of B VI (with 'added' sharpened sixth or chromatic neighbour note, E♮, it could also be F♯ VII⁷) is a typically ambiguous octatonic product and should not be assigned to a single function. Bar 5 introduces a C♯7 chord with a root outside the octatonic collection and a series of F♯ V–II⁷ progressions signalling a move to that tonal region and scale but without a statement of the tonic triad (see Example 6b). The five pitches common to the octatonic and F♯ collections are the most influential pitch classes in the course of the piece so far and form a connection as important as the functional relationship between B and its dominant.

A hexachord from another octatonic collection (B♭, C, C♯, D♯, E, F♯, G, A) generates the chordal progression in bars 8–9: non-resolving, non-functioning seventh chords (minor, major, diminished and half-diminished) are all consonances natural to octatonic writing. Four of each type occur in every octatonic scale, but without their normal chords of resolution (a dominant–tonic relationship is impossible in this type of scale). The A7 chord in bar 8 has nothing to do with D major; indeed, any sense of movement to D is scotched by the half-diminished seventh which follows: D♯–F♯–A–C♯; a typical octatonic progression between roots a tritone apart. This new collection shares a pentachord with the scale of E major which arrives in bar 10, only to be displaced by a suggestion of F♯ V. We then return to the opening collection, and B priority in bars 11–12. In bar 13, we find the non-octatonic hexachord 6–Z19:[2, 3, 5, 6, 10, 11] mentioned in the above discussion of 'Gnomus' (see Example 6c). This set is later used to construct the final two bars of the piece.

'Tuileries' is centred on B, but this arises from contextual emphasis rather than tonal function. Shifts between diatonic, octatonic and other types of collection serve both to articulate and to provide connections between phrases. Within phrases, allegiance to various collections gives coherence to chordal progressions which might otherwise be dismissed as 'colouristic'. Musorgsky's interpenetration and juxtaposition of pitch collection with different and distinctive characters, while still very much in embryo in 'Gnomus' and 'Tuileries', looks forward to the music of both Stravinsky and Debussy. The assignment of different formal functions to different types of collections (for example, the exclusive use of 6–Z19 as an ending set in 'Tuileries') places him particularly close to the latter.[7]

69

Example 7. An analytical sketch of the last five pictures

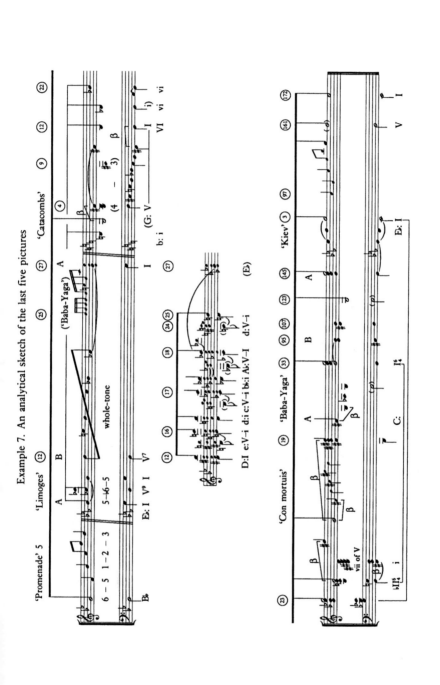

New linear structures

Several of the more diatonic, functional pictures ('Castello' is a good example) can be analysed using the Schenkerian method, typically prolonging a 5 4 3 2 1 *Ursatz*.[8] But these pieces do not interest us here, not least because to apply strict Schenkerian analysis to this work is to apply the wrong plot; it should not be judged by German standards or analysed in terms of German criteria even though doing so may be of theoretical interest. The opening 'Promenade' could easily be subjected to a Schenkerian analysis, but such a reading would force us to hear the piece as in B♭ from the beginning, depriving us of the wayward course to that tonic. Where linear analysis does come into its own is not in a strictly Schenkerian way but in more flexible modes appropriate to innovative passages where interesting methods of prolongation or, more accurately, association are employed.[9]

'Chicks' is a mixture of the conventional and unconventional.[10] The piece begins with a tonic (F) triad with the fifth uppermost prolonged by a German sixth, suggesting that a strict Schenkerian reading with primary tone 5 and a typical move to ♭6 (bars 21–2) might be possible. However, while the dominant, C, is broadly in control of bars 5–8 the material in between seems to be less a prolongation than a free connection in which, as Salzer points out, sonority (including parallel fifths) is more important than chord grammar. Furthermore, there are octatonic qualities here: the first and second and sixth to eighth chords are all drawn from a single octatonic collection with the middle three from another.

The similar, but longer, passage (bars 13–20) also suggests association, connection and interest in sonority rather than prolongation. Its course from the German sixth chord in bar 12 to the dominant in bar 20 is even more circuitous. The C major triad at the end of bar 20 and the ♭6–5 motion do not strike us as goals of the previous motion; indeed, the D♭/C figure seems more like an interruption. The inexactness of the broadly sequential writing, which owes nothing to the qualities of any underlying diatonic scale, also weakens the sense of direction. This passage has a quite different, whole-tone harmonic quality compared with the earlier one.

This chapter concludes with an examination of the final four pictures in conjunction with Example 7. The example summarises the linear structures within these pieces and draws attention to some important connections between them. The important role of the pitch G is shown by the beam, and its frequent association with F♯ is highlighted (see the motif designated 'beta').

71

The pitches B♭ and B (= C♭) also play a significant role in 'Limoges' and 'Catacombs'.

The fifth 'Promenade' is a dominant preparation for the return of E♭ in 'Limoges'. From here on there is a powerful sense of harmonic and linear integration, culminating in 'Kiev'. 'Limoges' is a fascinating mixture of diatonic and whole-tone prolongations on different structural levels. Its outer sections are firmly in E♭ with an emphasis on the fifth and ♭6 (as a member of V⁹). The central section prolongs the leading note D which is briefly tonicised in the major (bars 12–14) and minor at the foretaste of the 'Baba-Yaga' idea (bars 25–6). This prolongation is effected by a whole-tone motion marked by the triads on D, E, D, C, B♭, A♭ in bars 12, 14, 16, 17, 18 and 19. This whole-tone line uses the same collection as the whole-tone hoots and calls in bars 12–14 and 20–3; together they give the impression of an underlying altered (whole-tone) dominant seventh in which the line unfolds the crucial interval D/A♭ which resolves at the beginning of the final section. On the surface each triad in the whole-tone line is approached by its own dominant. So E♭ diatony prevails in the background, the middleground falls under a whole-tone influence and the surface mixes both diatonic and whole-tone features. Only by understanding the interaction of the dominant seventh and whole-tone writing are we able to make sense of this piece.

'Catacombs' is undoubtedly the strangest piece in the set, not least from the point of view of its harmony.[11] To understand it we must be sensitive to the tonal ambiguities which arise from the differing attractions of the linear and harmonic structures. 'Catacombs' is notated without key signature. The principal ambiguity is between G and B, which gives way to one between F♯ and B that persists through 'Con mortuis'. B = C♭ is the flattened submediant of E♭ and was prominent in that role in 'Limoges'. G is both the flattened submediant of B and the flattened supertonic of F♯, a pivotal role taken up in 'Con mortuis'. Also, when a move towards B is taken in bars 24–5 of 'Catacombs' it is via C major = B ♭II.

Almost devoid of melody, 'Catacombs' consists of stark chords contrasted in register, dynamic and spacing. The first chord after the opening unison statements of B and G fuses G major and B minor triads (creating a form of pitch-class set 4–20, a sonority referred to in 'Gnomus') in a way that makes it uncertain whether F♯ or G is the essential note; the situation is not clarified by the harmonies that follow. In the long run it transpires that F♯ is the primary tone (5 in B minor), but it takes us until the beginning of 'Con mortuis', where F♯ becomes a high pedal, to realise this. In the short term the progression in bars 4–11 reaches an F♯ triad but without major or minor third. This apparent dominant of B is contradicted by the linear structure in the bass. In bars 1–3 the bass outlines G major, in bars 4–11 its dominant D, with third F♯ in the upper voice. The bass-line descent fills the first interval in the arpeggiation (i.e. D–A) chromatically, and a full D triad occurs as A is reached in bar 9 (the inner voice G♮ in bars 6–8 sounding as though it has resolved 4–3). Musorgsky's dynamics emphasise the strange dissonant chord in bar 8 rather than the chord on A, the intermediate goal of this bass progression, in bar 9.

If a balance between B minor and G major is maintained throughout bars 1–11, bars 12–22 come down decisively in favour of G major, then minor, with a deviation to the dominant and dominant minor in bars 15–18 (note the incongruous, archaic 4–3 suspension in bars 15–16). The passage ends with an extraordinary cadence in G minor in which the bass fails to resolve A to G for nearly two bars. The sequence of chords that follows (E♭ major, C major, F♯7) is susceptible to a number of interpretations. Puffett explains the first two chords as a double Neapolitan (the E♭ relating back to the momentary D minor in bar 18 and the C major bearing a Neapolitan relationship to the overall key of B) resolving to the dominant in bar 25. However, the relationship between E♭ and D minor seems tenuous. The E♭ triad is certainly an advance reference to 'Kiev', it has that piece's primary tone, G, uppermost and in the bass. The progression E♭–C major reverses the keys of the final two pictures. Also the entire passage from bar 22 (last beat) to bar 25 exhibits a typically octatonic progression through triads with roots a minor third apart. Bars 25–7 prolong B V$^9_7$ but we end with B minor I$^6_4$ overlaid by a F♯ vii^7. On balance this chord favours resolution to F♯ rather than B.

'Con mortuis' is less complicated harmonically, but preserves the ambiguity between B and F♯. Progressions of three or four chords seem to gravitate now one way and then the other. The combination of the F♯ Neapolitan and the upper-voice pedal on the downbeat of bar 2 returns us once again to the 4–20 sonority. German sixth chords in F♯ (which as at the beginning of 'Chicks' progress directly to I) create a strong sense of F♯ in bars 11–14. B major then emerges in the left hand as F♯ persists in the right, creating Stravinskian sonorities. At the end the F♯ inverted pedal continues to sound and, although the harmony finally changes to B major, we are still uncertain as to whether F♯ or B has the upper hand.

Any analysis of these two linked pieces should be wary of reinterpreting the ambiguities in the light of the ultimate ending in B. At the beginning B and G seem to be in equilibrium, as do F♯ and B later. To reinterpret the whole in the light of the end and to decide that the beginning is really in B and the other elements are prolongational is to exclude a layer of meaning. B grows out of the opening and subsequent material, rather than being implicit from the beginning at a deeper level. Musorgsky often needs to be listened to linearly rather than in structural levels.

'Baba-Yaga' takes the F♯ prolonged throughout the previous piece and turns it into the leading note of G, recalling the close relationship between these pitch-classes in the preceding piece. 'Baba-Yaga' is ambiguous; while the key signature is C the contextual emphasis on G is very strong, and there are few clear progressions defining C.[12] At the beginning are the reiterated G's dominants or tonics? Should we hear A♭ as ♭2 or ♭6? The fierce ostinatos of bars 17–24 outline the diminished fifths G/D♭ and A/E♭, creating a whole-tone tetrachord. C triads are reached in bars 25 and 27 but in second inversion and at the beginnings of little non-functional I→II–II⁷→III progressions very similar to the passages discussed in 'Chicks'. Extensive use of I_4^6 as the witch flies (bars 33–9) begins to convince us of the supremacy of C. But the powerful, intrusive G minor VII⁷→VI progressions in bars 41 to 48 divert us back to G only to be interrupted by non-functional 'dominant' sevenths on B and C before C is restored in bars 55–6. The whole passage (bars 41–56) is bound together by the arresting whole-tone trichord F♯, B♭, C presented by the held notes in the tenor. The long preparation for the central section mostly outlines E♭ and G triads. Are these ♭VI and I or ♭III and V? The argument seems to come down in favour of C with the dominant ninth in bars 74–5, but then we find the passage ending with a strong contextual emphasis on G.

G is prolonged in the central section by an innovative linear structure. The two sections, bars 95–107 and 108–22, each move from an incomplete diminished seventh (A♯–(C♯)–E–G) to an augmented triad (B–D♯–G), with G as linking invariant. On both occasions the two chords are joined by a descending series of tremolo thirds which move from minor to major reflecting the intervallic qualities of the diminished seventh at one end and the augmented triad at the other. The descent is extended in bars 119–21 by a series of augmented triads. During the course of the passage localised moves to B (bar 112) and A (bar 116) resolving the diminished sevenths preceding them are subsidiary to the overall linear structure. In the early part of each passage a tension develops between right-hand interval structures – essentially based on minor thirds and semitones – and the left-hand melody built from whole tones and major thirds. Contrastingly, at the end of this section, whole-tone augmented triads progress in semitonal steps. The process is summarised in Example 7.

As already discussed, the most interesting harmonic and linear aspects of 'Kiev' are determined by folk, church and bell influences. The harmonisation of the main processional theme is straightforward. What is of interest here is how G – which has increasingly gained in status since the fifth 'Promenade', becomes the primary tone and is prolonged throughout the piece – is finally taken down to E♭ in the concluding bars.[13]

8

Orchestrations and transcriptions of 'Pictures at an Exhibition'

Pictures is probably the most often orchestrated and arranged work in the repertoire. These colourful and sometimes powerful pieces with their unsympathetic writing for the piano have left the feeling that the work should be orchestrated, but there is no evidence that Musorgsky ever planned to do so. The problems of orchestrating *Pictures* are many. While stylistic faithfulness to Musorgsky's own orchestral style might be desirable, his meagre orchestral output gives little guidance. There are also more specific problems such as coping with the large amount of dense low-register writing or with rapid pieces entirely in high registers. There is extensive use of unison and hollow two-part writing and the orchestrator also has to deal with the occasional appearances of virtuosic piano figuration and material which seems to be vocal rather than instrumental in conception. This chapter considers the principal transcriptions for serious concert performance. Many more exist, including the well-known rock one by Emmerson, Lake and Palmer. Some, such as the electronic realisation by Tomita, are clearly verging on bad taste. Musorgsky's original text may not be immutable, but what is added should provide us with new insights and be of the highest artistic and technical quality.

The history of orchestrating this work begins with the little-known composer and conductor Michael Touschmaloff (1861–96). Touschmaloff probably worked on his orchestration in 1886 (the year in which the Bessel edition of *Pictures* appeared) as a student in Rimsky-Korsakov's composition class. The orchestration was not performed until 1891, when it was given by his teacher. The Kalmus reprint of the score originally published by Bessel (1900) states that Rimsky-Korsakov 'collaborated' with Touschmaloff, but the truth is probably that his teacher is mentioned in an attempt to sell more copies. The orchestration shows little evidence of Rimsky-Korsakov's orchestral imagination. Abraham records that Anatol Lyadov (1855–1914), who impressed Musorgsky, contemplated making an orchestration in 1903; perhaps this too was at the suggestion of Rimsky-Korsakov, to whom he was close.[1] The indolent Lyadov seems never to have got round to the task.

The orchestration by Sir Henry Wood (1869–1944) dates from 1915, just after the Augener score appeared in London. He was encouraged to make it by his friend and expert on Russian music Rosa Newmarch.[2] Wood's orchestration was played quite frequently in the 1920s, but he banned performances from the early 1930s in deference to the Ravel version which he must have realised was not only a masterpiece, but was more respectful to Musorgsky than his own. With the death of Sir Henry's widow in 1977 public performance is again possible. In July 1922, just months before Ravel's orchestration appeared, one was produced by Leo Funtek (1885–1965). Funtek spent his working life mainly in Finland, notably as conductor of the Finnish Opera. His orchestration strongly contrasts with Wood's and, to a lesser extent, Ravel's in his almost absolute faithfulness to Musorgsky's original.

It seems that Ravel and Funtek were unaware that they were both transcribing the same piece at the same time. Ravel's orchestration (which we discuss in detail below) came as the result of a commission in 1920 from the wealthy Russian-born conductor Sergey Koussevitzky (1874–1951) for an orchestration in the manner of Rimsky-Korsakov for his orchestra's Paris concert series. The première took place on 19 October 1922. Prompted by Koussevitzky's confinement of the Ravel orchestration to his own use until 1929, Bessel commissioned a sumptuous alternative from the conductor Leonidas Leonardi first performed in Paris in 1925. This orchestration seems to have been a flop and after disappearing for a number of years has now partially re-emerged in Slatkin's compilation suite (see p. 86). When the Ravel arrangement was released from Koussevitzky's grip the royalties charged remained enormous. The Philadelphia Orchestra instructed their bass clarinettist and staff arranger Lucien Cailliet (1891–1984; composer of the score for Cecil B. De Mille's film *The Ten Commandments*) to produce an orchestration that avoided some of Ravel's effects. Perhaps the Philadelphia were afraid of litigation! Cailliet's orchestration was premièred by Ormandy in 1937. The Philadelphia remained faithful to this extremely competent arrangement for many years, only performing the Ravel occasionally with guest conductors. It finally fell into disuse in 1952.

The English born, naturalised American conductor Leopold Stokowski's (1882–1977) 'Symphonic Transcription' dates from 1938, just a year after Cailliet's. It is said that some of Stokowski's arrangements were substantially the work of Cailliet (whose period with the Philadelphia coincided with Stokowski's conductorship) and others, but it is probably true that Stokowski was so much in control that his assistants were essentially copyists. Undoubtedly Cailliet helped with Stokowski's *Pictures*, but the two men's orchestrations are on completely different wavelengths. Stokowski, a master orchestrator, transcribed nearly two hundred works by major eighteenth- and nineteenth-century composers. The freedom of his transcription technique is often criticised, but this is in part the result of the limitations of early recording techniques with their necessity to double, particularly in the woodwind. His orchestration of *Pictures* was quickly recorded on 78rpm discs.

Walter Goehr's (1903–60) orchestration appeared in 1942. It was intended for orchestras of flexible size, possibly to suit the exigencies of war-time Europe. In more recent years a rather different, yet eminently logical solution to the problems of orchestrating *Pictures* has appeared in the form of the as yet unperformed version for piano and orchestra by Lawrence Leonard (*b*.1926) completed in 1975.[3] Elgar Howarth's transcription for large brass ensemble (1979 and for brass band, 1981) ranks among the finest transcriptions even though the concerns of the arranger are with the technical difficulties of translating piano to brass and using the instruments in a way that is interesting and varied for the listener, rather than with enhancing or interpreting the qualities of the original. Furthermore, this work depends heavily on the virtuosity of the players, particularly in pieces which do not naturally lend themselves to brass, and was conceived with the potential of a particular group in mind (the Philip Jones Brass Ensemble).

Although a rather plain orchestration by Sergei Gorchakov (1905–76) appeared in the USSR in 1954, the first orchestration by a Russian-born musician of real stature is that by Vladimir Ashkenazy (*b*.1937) (who has also performed *Pictures* as a pianist and collaborated on the definitive Vienna Urtext Edition). The orchestration appeared in 1982. Ashkenazy considered Ravel's version too 'highly perfumed and insufficiently Russian'. His intention was to eschew effect for its own sake and to produce an orchestration 'guided by the deeper undercurrents of this predominantly dark-coloured piece. I have tried to work from within the music rather than from without'.[4]

In the first orchestration of *Pictures* Touschmaloff employed the standard late Romantic orchestra: triple woodwind (but two bassoons), four horns, two trumpets, three trombones, tuba, harp, percussion (including piano) and strings. Modest augmentations of this ensemble have become almost standard. The orchestrations by Ravel, Cailliet, Ashkenazy and Gorchakov are for this ensemble plus contra bassoon and an extra trumpet (or two in Wood's and Cailliet's orchestrations). Cailliet and Ashkenazy both make effective use of an E♭ clarinet, Wood an offstage euphonium (for 'Bydlo'). Ravel introduces the alto saxophone and Gorchakov a soprano saxophone (not for the troubadour but for Schmuÿle's whinging). Funtek, despite the plainness of his orchestration, requires quadruple flutes, clarinets and trombones and six horns, and Stokowski (typically) requires the largest combination of all the extant orchestrations with quadruple wind, eight horns and alto saxophone. Leonardi is reputed to have scored for vast forces including three saxophones. Wood, Stokowski and Goehr all call for that most un-Russian of instruments: the organ. Most of the orchestrations make use of tuned percussion including celeste. Percussion sections are always extensive; Ravel includes such devices as rattle and whip (later to be strikingly used in the finale of his Piano Concerto in G). Some orchestrators, notably Wood and Funtek, make effective use of chamber groups for pieces such as 'Tuileries'.

Ravel's orchestration

The First World War and the death of his mother had deeply depressed Ravel. This, and Diaghilev's rejection of *La Valse* (completed in 1920), had caused him increasingly to interest himself in transcription rather than original composition. Most of Ravel's major orchestral works started life as piano pieces, and transcription was almost second nature to him; the detached craftsmanship and concern with polish and perfection that it necessitated greatly appealed to the reclusive Ravel. In addition to orchestrating *Pictures* and works by Chabrier and Debussy at this time, he had also orchestrated his own *Le Tombeau de Couperin* in 1920. This was not the first time Ravel had worked on Musorgsky; he and Stravinsky had, at Diaghilev's instigation, collaborated on a now lost completion of *Khovanshchina*. The detached Ravel, affecting indifference, with his creed of art for arts sake and idolisation of Mozart, is the reverse of the Populist-realist Musorgsky. But there are some striking parallels. Neither man ever married and their sexual make-up is a mystery. Both lived rather isolated lives; both shared artistic fascinations with childhood, animals, fantasy and fairy-tale. So it is not surprising that the scenes in *Pictures* appealed to Ravel. He was probably fascinated too by Musorgsky's Russian portrayal of French scenes. Ravel was the master craftsman of the sonic moment, every sound is perfectly placed and scored, but despite his lack of 'patience with clumsiness and crudeness of technique' he appears not to have found any fault with Musorgsky's music. Indeed, he 'was very much influenced by Musorgsky in matters of texture, harmony and declamation'.[5]

Preferring *Boris Godunov* in the original version to that of Rimsky-Korsakov he attempted to obtain the original score of *Pictures*. 'I was expecting a copy of "Pictures at an Exhibition" in Musorgsky's original, and have just heard that it is unprocurable.'[6] He asked if his friend Michael Calvocoressi could help, but the best he could produce was the Rimsky-Korsakov version which he sent to Ravel in February 1922. In terms of cuts and additions Ravel's orchestration is quite faithful to Musorgsky. Apart from the omission of 'Promenade' 5, two additional bars of trumpet are added at the end of the first section of 'Baba-Yaga' and extra bars are added in 'Kiev' to cope with the increased resonance and power of the orchestra. Bars 21–2 of 'Chicks' are cut in the reprise so as to avoid repeating the shriek figure. Some octave doublings are added, but Ravel is remarkably restrained in̄ this respect. The obvious mistakes in the Rimsky-Korsakov edition are corrected but flaws such as the lack of *attacca* markings and the crescendo at the beginning of 'Bydlo' remain. However, in terms of altering attacks and dynamics and introducing marks of articulation, Ravel adds a whole new layer to Musorgsky.

While in his transcriptions details of dynamic, articulation and phrasing are added meticulously, Ravel might, with typical detachment, remove instructions with regard to expression. In *Pictures* only the barest titles are given, with some markings being simplified (in 'Castello' *Andantino molto cantabile e dolore* becomes simply *Andante*, in 'Goldenberg' *Grave energico* is removed after the opening *Andante*). However, Ravel does not go as far as in some of his other transcriptions where he replaces verbal markings with bare metronome marks.

Ravel remarked to Calvocoressi that his orchestration of *Pictures* 'used all possible ingredients'.[7] Devices such as glissando, flutter-tonguing and muting are widespread and the instrumental combinations are sometimes exotic. In the strings Ravel typically pays close attention to the distribution of parts, to bowing, articulation, open strings, double stopping and pizzicato and he utilises various effects. For example, in 'Gnomus' we hear glissandos to harmonics bowed over the fingerboard at Figure 9 and the use of portamento later on. In 'Castello' we find eight-part strings with first violins both muted and divided at Figure 29. At the end of 'Con Mortuis' the strings are richly divided with harmonics in first cellos and first basses (the prominent harp homophones here are typical of this instrument's prominence throughout the orchestration; harp harmonics also occur in numerous places).

Many places in Musorgsky's score suggest the use of brass. Ravel's writing is striking for its restraint in using the full brass choir, and for the care with which he balances and interlocks lines. The vocal quality of trumpet and brass choir ideally conveys the sense of solo and chorus in the opening 'Promenade' and the ceremonial associations of the trumpet are in keeping with the opening of the exhibition. Ravel's orchestrations use trombones extremely sparingly. The opening 'Promenade' excludes second trombone and only introduces the first at the very end. In 'Bydlo' trumpets and trombones are excluded from the climax; how easy it would have been for a less sensitive orchestrator automatically to write parts for them.

Flutter-tonguing and muting are frequently employed. Muted trumpet is often required, most noticeably for Schmuÿle's whinging. This passage is a masterstroke: a seventeen-bar exercise in continuous triple-tonguing with little room to breathe (unless, as often happens, first and second players alternate); not only is the music transcribed but its virtuosity too. In 'Bydlo' we have the inspired choice of the tuba for the lumbering solo. The tuba Ravel has in mind here is certainly not the heavy bass instrument, but a smaller, less gruff French one (the heavy bass tuba has only very recently been introduced into French orchestras). Rimsky-Korsakov's crescendo at the beginning of 'Bydlo' is stunningly orchestrated by Ravel, but it moves us even further from Musorgsky's intended sudden opening 'right between the eyes' (see p. 40).

In 'Castello', Musorgsky's troubadour, with his strong Russian accent, sings to the highly evocative and French sound of the alto saxophone. This instrument found more favour in France than elsewhere, notably in Bizet's *L'Arlésienne*, and it is from this line of orchestration that the solo comes rather than from jazz, where it was only beginning to establish itself at that time. A little later the saxophone was to become important to Russian composers, notably Prokofiev and Glazunov. An extra bar is added at the end to give the saxophone more time to die away: a moment to savour at every performance.

For Ravel, Musorgsky's use of dynamics, accents and phrase marks must have lacked discrimination. He creates a much more differentiated range of accents by using a variety of attacks and highly selective orchestral doublings (particularly with percussion) to point individual notes and rhythms, and he introduces more gradation into Musorgsky's dynamics. His treatment of 'Gnomus' is typical. Musorgsky makes excessive use of *sforzando* in the first thirty-seven bars. Ravel introduces a much wider and more refined selection of dynamics providing more subtle contrasts (as in the contrast of normal and muted horns at the beginning). In the reworked repeat of bars 19–28 Ravel introduces contrasts of colour (muted tuba counterpointed by woodwind being replaced by bass clarinet and celeste) and dynamics where none existed in Musorgsky. The original *sforzandos* are replaced by a wide variety of carefully calculated bodies of pizzicato strings, harp harmonics and percussion. Restricting the dynamics at Figures 8 and 9 allows more forcible outbreaks when they are really needed, as when the aggressive B♭ returns two bars before Figure 9.

In 'Tuileries' a new expressive layer is added by Ravel's crescendos in bars

7–9 and 22–4 which rise sharply to *fortissimo* like the outburst of a persistent child's temper. In 'Limoges', another piece which Musorgsky indiscriminately scatters with *sforzandos*, Ravel moulds and shapes with a wider range of dynamics, marks of accentuation and, importantly, percussion (for example, the side drum draws out the rhythm of Musorgsky's *sforzandos* in bars 4 and 24). The use of percussion to propel this piece to its conclusion is a feature also found at the end of 'Gnomus' and 'Baba-Yaga'. In the latter piece, Musorgsky's dynamics are reorganised to allow the building of orchestral paragraphs. Musorgsky intended bar 25 to be *forte*, but Ravel introduces a sudden *piano* here to allow a crescendo to build to the ride of the witch in bar 33. The lowest bass register is removed until that point which is also where the powerful trumpets are introduced.

Antiphonal writing, first found in the ninth bar of the first 'Promenade' when brass are replaced by strings, is a particular feature of the 'Promenades'. It is most starkly to the fore when the groups of trombones alternating with horns (sometimes hand-stopped) and bassoons in 'Catacombs' are replaced by strings and woodwind in 'Con Mortuis' with its return of the 'Promenade' idea. However, Ravel's contrasts are usually more subtle because, unlike his Russian counterparts, he tends not to favour primary orchestral colours. So, for example, when he writes for the slithering bass clarinet in the final section of 'Gnomus' he further colours it with double-bass trills and cello glissandos. When the oboe appears at the beginning of 'Tuileries' it is doubled with the flute; the oboe is legato, the flute legato staccato, possibly in an attempt to imitate the French *stile perle* piano playing.[8] Ravel's tendency to double woodwind and his fussy articulation does make 'Tuileries' less playful than it might be. 'Limoges', although echoing the bustle of the market place, is similarly fussy and heavily doubled. The strings constantly shift from unison to *divisi*, arco to pizzicato and the wind busily draw out and toss around little fragments. Sometimes this is to useful effect as when the wind draw out Musorgsky's forward reference to 'Baba-Yaga' in the woodwind.

The oboe is prominent in the pieces involving children: 'Tuileries' and 'Chicks'. The latter piece must have had a particular appeal for Ravel given his love of children, fantasy and dance. Musorgsky's high percussive piano writing is replaced with staccato woodwind and pizzicato strings. Individual notes are pointed by harp, high bassoon, pizzicato muted strings and cymbal. Six woodwind players (*fortissimo*) take the final scream, but playfully allow only the two flutes the final C. In the trio Ravel's orchestration of the ostinato-like patterns creates layers of distinct rhythms and timbres (muted violin trills, leaping bassoon, narrow-range viola with pizzicato ostinato, horn pedal and so forth) that increase in number creating a crescendo of busyness in a manner reminiscent of Stravinsky. The layers are many and varied. We note particularly the resourceful way Ravel scores the F pedals. These only appear in two octaves in Musorgsky, but Ravel adds more. The F's appear flutter-tongued in the flute, as repeated (f^4) quavers with acciaccaturas in the piccolo, as repeated horn notes, as harp harmonics, as oboe leaping octave semiquavers, as bassoon offbeats and so on.[9] We also notice how the horn and side drum link the reorchestrated repeats of each half of the trio.

Some remarks on the other transcriptions

Brilliant as they are, Ravel's solutions to the problems of orchestrating *Pictures* are not the only ones, even if their familiarity makes them seem so. Ravel's trumpet at the opening or the saxophone in 'Castello' are masterstrokes, but we should not reject more Musorgskian possibilities such as the strings and woodwind at the beginning of Funtek's transcription. However, even if Ravel's orchestration is regarded as too decorative and French, its high level of inspiration cannot be doubted, a quality clearly lacking from Touschmaloff's workman-like orchestration. Touschmaloff's Russian darkness is apparent from the opening where clarinets double strings. There are echoes of Tchaikovsky in 'Chicks' and in the rapid articulation required in the woodwind in the second part of 'Goldenberg' and in 'Limoges'. His bell passage in 'Kiev' is more effectively Russian than Ravel's (whose tendency to smooth and blend prevents him from clearly articulating the layers of sound). Touschmaloff does not set the complete work. 'Gnomus', 'Tuileries', 'Bydlo' and all the 'Promenades' except the fifth, which is placed at the beginning, are omitted. 'Castello' is transposed to G minor and the central section of 'Limoges' is inexplicably rewritten.

Wood too preserves only the opening 'Promenade'; the reprise in 'Baba-Yaga' is cut and replaced by eleven bars of dissonant offstage bells. 'Kiev' is transposed to C major, destroying Musorgsky's key-scheme. As Klein points out, this may have been done to allow a 32' organ pedal C to sound at the end.[10] Unlike Touschmaloff, Wood introduces effects such as the offstage euphonium accompanied by a 'small Indian drum' in 'Castello' and the harp threaded with paper for a glissando at the end of the first section in 'Goldenberg'.

Funtek's orchestration has begun to attract more attention in an age that accords high respect to faithfulness to the composer's text. Funtek carefully preserves every detail of the (Rimsky-Korsakov) edition of the original. But it remains arguable that some flexibility must be allowed if the aim is genuinely to transcribe rather than simply to copy out for different instruments. Nevertheless, Funtek's orchestration is probably not far from what Musorgsky would have produced. The orchestration is sometimes unimaginative and over doubled in a manner reminiscent of late Schumann; some instrumental choices such as the bass clarinet in the 'Bydlo' theme are misjudged. But Funtek's sheer elemental power seems more appropriate than Ravel's polished perfection in, for example, 'Baba-Yaga'.

Cailliet's transcription is colourful and competent, but no more Russian than Ravel's and conceived with the sound of the Philadelphia Orchestra in mind. For example, his string writing suits the rather exaggerated legato style of Ormandy's Philadelphia and their frequent use of portamento. It makes liberal use of effects like harp harmonics, string glissandos and muted string and brass playing (probably the result both of Cailliet's origins as a French bandmaster and the influence of Ravel). Like Ravel, Cailliet feels it necessary to revise phrasing, dynamic and attack marks thoroughly.

Stokowski reworked Musorgsky's score into a showpiece whose distortions and exaggerations go beyond reason. His justification was that he found Ravel's orchestration too French; he desired a more Slavic character in which the changing moods were reflected by more powerfully contrasted colours.[11] Perhaps it was this quest for Russianness that led him to exclude 'Tuileries', 'Limoges' and their prefacing 'Promenades'. Other pieces are mercilessly altered and cut. 'Catacombs' is crushed into 4/2 bars, its harmony normalised, and glissandos and awesome crescendos added. The effect is apocalyptic rather than mysterious. Most of the original markings are modified and many additional ones added, some quite contrary to Musorgsky's intentions. In 'Kiev' the chorale melody's *senza espressione* becomes *Liberamente, sostenuto e legato, cantabile*. At the opening Musorgsky's 5/4 and 6/4 bars are divided 3/4, 2/4, 3/4, 3/4 destroying much of their flexibility and ambiguity.

Cailliet had already exaggerated Ravel's tendency towards antiphony; Stokowski takes this to extremes. He frequently and abruptly juxtaposes contrasting choirs of primary colours without a connecting sonority (the emphasis on primary colours necessitates much use of higher and lower members of wind families). When combining instruments each family tends to be allocated a line rather than blending and interlocking in Ravel's manner. Excess features strongly. The eight horns in unison at the opening of 'Gnomus' percussively marking the rhythm and then terrifyingly soaring through a tenth *crescendo molto* after Figure 1 or the enormous brass snarl in bars 35–7 are good examples. Effects are numerous. In the trio of 'Chicks' muted violins play both tremolos and trills simultaneously and flutes, only scored as trilled, both trill and flutter-tongue in the recording. The playful, cheeky melody in the second half of the trio becomes weird and fantastic when the strings replace Musorgsky's acciaccaturas with glissandos marked *sempre sul E, fantastico*.

Cutting and altering the sequence of pieces in *Pictures* can have some very undesirable effects. Having omitted 'Gnomus', Walter Goehr moves 'Limoges' forward leaving its upward rush at the end leading to an anticlimax: a solo viola at the beginning of the second 'Promenade'! Such problems do not occur in Ashkenazy's careful and complete orchestration. This is weightier, somewhat coarser and brassier than Ravel's. Its darker quality comes partly from the greater emphasis on clarinets and the lower registers of the brass (summed up in the final chord of the work where the trumpets are instructed to play at the very bottom of their compass). This is a more Russian orchestration and is in the spirit of the original, but it is sophisticated and goes beyond what Musorgsky could have achieved himself.

The tone is set at the opening, with three trumpets to Ravel's one, followed by a full *tutti*; virtually all the woodwind and strings are assigned to either the melody or bass line with the brass filling the harmony, giving an appropriate congregational effect. In this orchestration, colouring of line takes precedence over internal balance, blending and interlocking. Ashkenazy does not reject effects and the addition of small amounts of material. In 'Gnomus', Ravel's string glissandos are replaced by four muted double basses playing rapid ascending and descending chromatic scales in *divisi* thirds. The trio of 'Chicks' is given further layers of woodwind decoration, pizzicato arpeggios and so on. The dark oboe d'amore appears for the troubadour solo and a shivery, teeth-chattering solo violin takes Schmuÿle's melody.

'Tuileries', fast and light with minimal doublings, reflects Ashkenazy the pianist's view of this piece. Four horns blast forth *fortissimo* at the beginning of 'Bydlo': the first orchestration (except Howarth's brass version) to get this right. As Ravel and all good orchestrators realised the opening of 'Kiev' must be restrained. Ashkenazy's combination of wind and harps is very effective, providing appropriate grandeur while leaving large resources to be tapped later. The second chorale is scored for high horns; despite Ashkenazy's self-confessed desire to remain close to Musorgsky's intentions, his marking *molto espressivo* conflicts with Musorgsky's *senza espressione* here. His Russian upbringing enables him to cope with the bell sounds in 'Kiev' exceptionally well and an added pause bar allows the metallic percussion sounds to continue

85

to ring out. This orchestration, while not the consummate work of art that Ravel's is, effects a fitting compromise between faithfulness to the Russian original and imagination.

There are many other instrumentations that could be discussed ranging from those for symphonic band to accordion and guitar. Several arrangements for organ exist (notably by Wills and Camilleri although theoretically there are as many organ transcriptions as there are organs and organists). The organ might seem to offer a sensible solution to some of the problems of *Pictures* since it is a keyboard instrument with a much wider range of sonorities and infinite sustaining powers. But it is fundamentally un-Russian and simply cannot attack, phrase and shape in a way appropriate to Musorgsky. Furthermore, it tends to live in reverberant acoustics which blur the rapid detailed passages. These organ transcriptions are as much concerned with the qualities of particular instruments as they are with Musorgsky, and like so many transcriptions for solo instruments they exist as much to challenge the player as to enhance or throw new light upon the original.

Throughout this study we have sought to stress the originality and Russianness of Musorgsky's composition and its unique nature in the history of nineteenth-century music. At the end of the day it must be the strengths of the composition rather than its weaknesses as a piano work (most of which are more in the ears of those who hear the work from the wrong perspective than in the work itself) which have attracted others to refashion it. Even as I write the process continues and moves to a new phase: in 1991 the conductor Leonard Slatkin performed a 'compilation-suite' drawn from various transcriptions at, appropriately enough, a Henry Wood Promenade Concert; we are, as it were, moving to arrangements of arrangements.

Appendix

'Pictures at an Exhibition': principal transcriptions giving recordings where they are not in the current commercial catalogues

1 Touschmaloff, Michael (1886)
(London and New York, Edwin Kalmus)
Recorded on Acanta DC 22128

2 Wood, Henry (1915)
Unpublished. Score and parts held in Library of Royal Academy of Music in London, available on microfilm.

3 Funtek, Leo
Manuscript in Library of Helsinki Philharmonic Orchestra.
(Espoo, Finland, Musiikki Fazer 1990)
Recorded on Compact Disc

4 Ravel, Maurice (1922)
(London, Boosey & Hawkes and Eulenburg)
Numerous recordings.

5 Cailliet, Lucien (1937)
Unpublished. Score and parts in the Library of the Philadelphia Orchestra.
Recording on 78 rpm discs RCA Vic. 14851/4 (set M442)

6 Stokowski, Leopold (1938)
(New York, Peters Edition, 1971)
Recorded on London SPC 2111 and Decca VIV 26

7 Goehr, Walter (1942)
(London, Boosey & Hawkes)

8 Gorchakov, Sergei (1954)
(First Western performance by the Philadelphia Orchestra 10 April 1986, in Philadelphia)
Materials available in USA from Soviet Publishing Agency VAAP

9 Leonard, Lawrence (1975) [solo piano and orchestra]
(London, Boosey & Hawkes 1977)

10 Howarth, Elgar (1979) [for Brass Ensemble]
(London, Chester)
Recorded on Argo ZRG 885

10a Howarth, Elgar (1981) [for Brass Band]
(London, Chester)

11 Ashkenazy, Vladimir 198(4?)
Material available from Harrison Parrott Management, London. Publication is
under negotiation.

Note

The transcription by Leonidas Leonardi (Bessel, 1925) is very difficult to obtain. There is reputed
to be a transcription by Fabien Sevitzky, Koussevitzky's nephew, and conductor of the Indianapolis
Orchestra (1937-55); I am unable to verify the existence of this work. The undated arrangement
by Giuseppe Becce and Fr. Schimak published by Robert Lineau, Berlin (playable with a very small
group) and the various educational arrangements by Bloodworth, Carter, Stone and Herfurth once
available from Oxford University Press, do not stand serious comparison with the transcriptions
listed in the above appendix. I have not made any attempt to catalogue or study transcriptions of
parts of the work or arrangements for solo instruments and ensembles of diverse kinds up to and
including symphonic bands.

Notes

1 *Pictures* and nineteenth-century music

1 Olkhovsky, *Vladimir Stasov*, p. 46.
2 Written in response to a request from Hugo Riemann in 1880 for an entry for his music dictionary. Leyda and Bertensson, *Musorgsky Reader*, pp. 416–20.
3 Hübsch, *Modest Mussorgskij*, p. 10.
4 Garden, *Balakirev*, p. 317.
5 Edward Garden, 'Balakirev's influence on Musorgsky' in Brown, *Mikhail Glinka*, p. 19.
6 Leyda and Bertensson, *Musorgsky Reader*, p. 38.
7 For a full discussion of relationships between 'The Five' and the men of the St Petersburg Conservatory see Ridenour, *Nationalism*.
8 Leyda and Bertensson, *Musorgsky Reader*, p. 18.
9 For a much fuller discussion of these and subsequent issues see R. Hoops, 'Musorgsky and the Populist age' in Brown, *Musorgsky: In Memoriam*, and Stasov, 'Selected articles on Musorgsky'.
10 Edie *et al.*, *Russian Philosophy*, p. 3.
11 *Ibid.*, p. 111.
12 Musorgsky: autobiography in Leyda and Bertensson, *Musorgsky Reader*, pp. 416–20.
13 Edie *et al.*, *Russian Philosophy*, p. ix.
14 Leyda and Bertensson, *Musorgsky Reader*, p. 120.
15 Edie *et al.*, *Russian Philosophy*, p. 13. See Taruskin, 'Realism', on the subject of realism in the music of 'The Five'.
16 Leyda and Bertensson, *Musorgsky Reader*, p. 122.
17 On motion in realism see Calvocoressi, *Modest Mussorgsky*, p. 89.
18 Realism placed importance on accurate historical source materials, those with a message for nineteenth-century society having special significance.
19 Dahlhaus, *Realism*, p. 121.
20 *Ibid.*, p. 12.

2 Musorgsky and Hartman

1 To note 11, unless otherwise indicated, translated quotations from Musorgsky and others are from Orlova, *Musorgsky's Days and Works*.
2 Orlova's chronology is strange. The two reminiscences are dated March and spring, but her introduction tells us they did not share until the autumn.
3 Turner, 'Musorgsky', p. 154.
4 G. Abraham, 'The artist of *Pictures from an Exhibition*' in Brown, *Musorgsky: In Memoriam*, p. 234.
5 Vladimir Stasov, 'Hartman's exhibition', *Sankt-Peterburgskiye vedemosti*, 70 (12 March 1874).
6 *Victor Alexandrovich Hartman, Architect. A Biography and Catalogue of all his Works*, compiled by Nikolai Sobko, Secretary of the Society for the Promotion of Arts (St Petersburg, 1874).

89

7 A footnote in Vladimir Stasov, 'Musorgsky: biographical sketch' in *Vestnik Europy*, 5 and 6 (1881) trans. in Stasov, 'Selected articles'.

8 Orlova, *Musorgsky's Days and Works*, p. 24.

9 Leyda and Bertensson, *Musorgsky Reader*, pp. 274–5.

10 The principal source of information on Hartman is Stasov. English readers are fortunate in that much of his most pertinent writing has been translated in Frankenstein, 'Victor Hartman', and Abraham in Brown (see note 4). Frankenstein reproduces some Hartman pictures not used by Musorgsky in his article and in his valuable notes to the edition published by the International Music Company.

11 Schnitke, 'Pictures', p. 327.

12 Fried, Notes in Musorgsky, *Kartinki*, facsimile autograph.

13 The jug design is reproduced in the IMC Score.

14 Valkenier, *Russian Realist Art*, p. xi.

3 Manuscript, publication and performance

1 M. P. Musorgsky, *Kartinki s vystavski*, facsimile autograph (Moscow: USSR State Publishing House 'Muzyka', 1975).

2 Rimsky-Korsakov, *My Musical Life*, pp. 248–9.

3 Kreuz, 'Urtext' (Mainz, 1954).

4 The principal alterations made by Rimsky-Korsakov in addition to those discussed in the text include the omission of *attacca* markings after the 'Promenades' and 'Chicks'; extra and changed dynamic markings (principally *pianissimo* at the beginning of 'Bydlo') and tidying up Musorgsky's legato and staccato markings. No. 1, bar 34: C♮ on second quaver replaced with B♭ to make it analogous with bars 9 and 16. No. 2, bar 98: B♭ substituted for Musorgsky's tenor A♮, spoiling his chromatic descent (printing error?). No. 4, bar 24: first beat lengthened to a crotchet. No. 6: rhythmic changes at opening as discussed in text; bar 25: doubles bass F♯ in the tenor, omits C♮ in the next bar (printing error?); triplet upbeat to the final note, C–D–B♭ becomes C–D–C. 'Promenade' 5, bar 15: G substituted for B♭ in bass. 'Kiev', bar 6: first-inversion chord of B♭ rather than root position; bar 8: G minor chord for Musorgsky's B♭ major; bar 17: E♭ removed from the inner voices of the left hand (to lighten the texture or typographical error?); bar 30: melodic E♭ replaced with A♭ producing a smoother transition from the previous section; bars 114, 116, 118 and 119: right-hand chords thickened.

5 Reilly, *Music of Musorgsky*, pp. 32–3.

6 'Promenade' 2: opening *piano* missing; bar 10, fourth beat: ♮ missing from the D. No. 4: *pedante* instead of *pesante*. No. 7: bar 37, twenty-second demisemiquaver: D rather than E♭. No. 9, bar 53: A♮ rather than Musorgsky's F♯ in the tenor. No. 10, bar 35: F♭ missing; bar 60, inner voice: F rather than E♭; bar 101, third quaver: D rather than C in right hand; bar 166: left-hand pedal E♭'s are missing.

7 Montagu-Nathan, 'New Light on Moussorgsky's Pictures', p. 105.

8 Horowitz: LM 2357.

9 Brailowsky: Victor 18366/9; Moiseiwitsch: GC 3576/9; Horowitz: Victor 12-0489/92.

10 Richter presently on Compact Disc, Phillips 420-774-2.

11 *American Record Guide*, 34 (1968), p. 119.

4 Looking at Musorgsky's *Pictures*

1 See Chapter 2, note 7.

2 Leyda and Bertensson, *Musorgsky Reader*, p. 272.

3 Bobrovsky, 'Structural analysis', p. 151.

4 *Songs and Dances of Death* (1875) reflects *Pictures* in its employment of a variety of musical genre: lullaby, serenade, Russian dance and *Dies Irae* motif, concluding triumphal Russian and

Polish song. The juxtaposition of the grotesque and the comic with death and the Polish reference also link the two works.

5 Fried, Notes, p. 2.

6 I thank Edward Garden for drawing this to my attention.

5 Synopsis

1 Except where otherwise identified the references from Musorgsky refer to his letter to Stasov quoted on p. 17. Those of Stasov are conflated from the sources identified in Chapter 4 and his letter to Rimsky-Korsakov quoted on p. 18.

2 Brown, *Mikhail Glinka*, p. 228.

3 This and all further references Fried, Notes.

4 This and all other cut material in *Pictures* is reproduced in the Vienna Urtext Edition.

5 Hartman's sketch of the cathedral tower at Périgeux in France is an example of his work of this kind. See Frankenstein, 'Victor Hartman and Modeste Musorgsky', and the IMC score.

6 Leyda and Bertensson, *Musorgsky Reader*, pp. 133–4.

7 Newmarch, *Concert-Goer's Library*, p. 39.

8 Ashkenazy: note to the Vienna Urtext Edition.

9 Frankenstein, 'Victor Hartman and Modeste Musorgsky', p. 283.

10 Garden, *Balakirev*, p. 235.

11 Brown, *Mikhail Glinka*, p. 228.

12 Orlova, *Musorgsky's Days and Works*, p. 181.

13 In Frankenstein, 'Victor Hartman and Modeste Musorgsky', and the IMC score.

14 Leyda and Bertensson, *Musorgsky Reader*, pp. 82 and 394.

15 Schwartz, Boris, 'Musorgsky's interest in Judaica' in Brown, *Musorgsky: in Memoriam*, p. 91.

16 Frankenstein, 'Victor Hartman and Modeste Musorgsky', and the IMC score reproduce one of these of a 112-year-old woman in church.

17 Garden has linked this passage with a similar motif at the return of the Allegro molto in Balakirev's symphonic poem *In Bohemia* (1866–7).

18 In his article and in the IMC edition of the score Frankenstein reproduces a copy of this drawing from the magazine *Pchela* (No. 1, 1875). This is a copy by another artist who has attempted to fill in the missing detail and 'tidy up' Hartman.

19 Frankenstein, 'Victor Hartman and Modeste Musorgsky', pp. 287 and 274.

20 Forte, 'Musorgsky as modernist', p. 5.

21 Musorgsky's bell writing may owe something to the finale of Balakirev's unfinished E♭ major Piano Concerto begun in 1861–2. See Garden, *Balakirev*, pp. 258–9.

6 The musical language of *Pictures*

1 See Richard Taruskin, '*Little Star*: an etude in the folk style', in Brown, *Musorgsky: in Memoriam*.

2 In Lvov and Prác's collection (1790) and Rimsky-Korsakov's *100 Russian Folk Tunes* (1877). Rimsky-Korsakov used the tune in his *Overture on Russian Themes* (1866), Beethoven had made use of the tune in his String Quartet Op. 59 no. 2.

3 Hübsch, *Modest Mussorgskij*, p. 13. Compare 'The Crane', a Ukrainian tune used in Tchaikovsky's Second Symphony, with 'Promenade' and 'Kiev'.

4 Swan, *Russian Music*, p. 25.

5 Vladimir Morosan, 'Musorgsky's choral style' in Brown, *Musorgsky: in Memoriam*, pp. 105 and 99.

6 Swan, *Russian Music*, p. 27 (from Listopadov's collection of Don Cossack songs of 1911).

7 Calvocoressi, *Modest Mussorgsky*, p. 2.

8 Morosan in Brown, *Musorgsky: in Memoriam*, p. 117.

9   See Leyda and Bertensson, *Musorgsky Reader*, p. 417 n.
10 A. Tcherepnin, *Anthology of Russian Music* (Bonn, 1966), quoted in Hübsch, *Modest Mussorgskij*, p. 37.
11 Morosan, 'Musorgsky's choral style', p. 123 and his Example 36b from Bortniansky.
12 *Sobraniye sochineny* (St Petersburg, 1894), Vol. 3, p. 600 translated Brown, *Mikhail Glinka*.
13 Swan, 'The nature of Russian folk-song', p. 508.

7 Harmony, scales, tonality and voice-leading

1   See Michael Russ, 'The mysterious thread in Musorgsky's *Nursery*', *Music Analysis*, 9 (1990), pp. 47–66.
2   Forte, 'Musorgsky as modernist', pp. 3–46.
3   See Allen Forte, *The Structure of Atonal Music* (New Haven and London, 1973). Using the idea of the pitch-class set, Forte developed a method of classifying all the possible horizontal and vertical pitch combinations. All tones are regarded as one of twelve pitch classes, so C♮/B♯/D♭♭, in whatever register, are all forms of pitch-class 0. C♯/D♭ = pitch-class 1, D♮/C×/E♭♭ = 2 and so on. Pitch classes combine to form pitch-class sets of which there are 208 possibilities (excluding sets of only one pitch class or the unwieldy eleven pitch-class set). Sets are unordered groupings without internal hierarchies and are subject to both transposition and inversion, they are consequently deployed in many different ways in compositions. They are classified such that the left-hand 'cardinal' number represents the number of (different) pitch classes in the set, and the right-hand number its class number according to its position on Forte's list (pp. 177–88) which is ordered according to the interval content of sets. Sets with the designation 'Z' have the special quality that while being made up of different groups of pitch classes they have the same interval vector (a count of the intervals possible between every pair of pitch classes in the set) as some other set of the same size.
4   A group of pitches is symmetrical if it can be disposed in a balanced manner about an axis which may, or may not, be a member of the group. Furthermore, axes never occur singly but always in a tritone-related pair. For example, the set 4–7: [2, 3, 10, 11] at the opening can be symmetrically disposed about the axes 6/7 or 0/1.
5   Forte, 'Musorgsky as modernist', pp. 13–18.
6   An octatonic scale (Messiaen's second mode of limited transposition) is an eight-note scale of alternating whole tones and semitones. Being symmetrical it has only three distinct forms, just as the whole-tone scale exists in only two. For a fine account of its origins and use in nineteenth-century Russian music see Taruskin, 'Chernomor to Kashchei'.
7   See P. C. Van den Toorn, *The Music of Igor Stravinsky* (New Haven and London, 1983) and R. S. Parks, *The Music of Claude Debussy* (New Haven and London, 1989).
8   Schenkerian analysis (after Heinrich Schenker, 1868–1935) conceives tonal music (particularly that of the German masters) in terms of structural levels each controlled by the principles of strict counterpoint and figured bass. At each structural level decisions with regard to structural importance are made according to these rules until, by the process of reducing-out the inessential material, the *Ursatz* or fundamental structure is reached (a diatonic underlying projection of the tonic triad). The concept of prolongation (see note 9) is fundamental to this kind of analysis. The bulk of a work will be assumed to prolong a primary tone, the first tone of the fundamental structure (normally the third or fifth of the tonic triad) before closure is effected by final descent to the tonic. In Schenkerian analysis graphs are constructed in which rhythmic values indicate structural importance rather than duration.
9   Prolongation in its strictest sense is the process whereby a tone or harmony may be in structural control whilst not actually present. At all points in a prolongation what is prolonged and what is prolonging should be clear. When there is uncertainty with regard to this issue it is best to invoke broader concepts such as association.

10 A partial voice-leading analysis of this piece comes in Felix Salzer, *Structural Hearing* (New York, 1962), Vol. II, p. 192.
11 For a fascinating analysis of this piece see Puffett, 'Graphic analysis'.
12 If one were to take G as the tonic, then from 'Limoges' the work would divide the octave into descending major thirds: Eb, B, G, Eb.
13 Puffett, 'Graphic analysis'.

8 Orchestrations and transcriptions

1 Abraham in Calvocoressi/rev. Abraham, *Mussorgsky*, p. 174 n.
2 Wood's arrangement is discussed in Newmarch, *Concert-Goer's Library*, pp. 38–41.
3 Although Leonard carried out some careful editorial work, the lack of a reliable Urtext in 1975 still resulted in inaccuracies like 'Bydlo' beginning *piano*.
4 Ashkenazy: remarks from BBC Radio talk (1989) and Compact Disc notes (Decca 414 386–2).
5 Calvocoressi, 'From my note book' (1938), p. 202.
6 Letter to Calvocoressi in Calvocoressi, 'Ravel's letters', p.11.
7 Calvocoressi, 'From my note book' (1938), p. 202.
8 See J. A. Diaz, 'A Pedagogical Study for Oboe of Four Orchestral Works by Ravel' (diss., U. of Texas at Austin, 1988).
9 The held Ab in the viola at Figure 53 in the Hawkes full and pocket scores should surely be F.
10 For comparison and discussion of most of the orchestrations see Klein, 'Musorgsky's *Pictures*'.
11 Stokowski indicates his attitudes to orchestrating this work in the notes to the 78 rpm recording.

Select bibliography

Abraham, Gerald. 'Musorgsky' in *The New Grove Dictionary of Music and Musicians*, ed. Stanley Sadie (London, 1980)

Bird, Alan. *A History of Russian Painting* (Oxford, 1987)

Bobrovsky, V. 'A structural analysis of Musorgsky's Pictures from an Exhibition', in *From Lully to our Days* (Moscow, 1967) [in Russian only]

Brown, David. *Mikhail Glinka* (London, 1974)

Brown, Malcolm Hamrick (ed.). *Musorgsky: in Memoriam 1881–1981* (Ann Arbor, 1982)

Calvocoressi, Michael D. 'From my note book', *Musical Opinion*, 61 (1937), pp. 15-16

'From my note book', *Musical Opinion*, 62 (1938), pp. 202–3

'Ravel's letters to Calvocoressi', *Musical Quarterly*, 27 (1941), pp. 1–9

'When Ravel composed to order', *Music and Letters*, 22 (1941), pp. 54–9

Mussorgsky (London, 1946, rev. Gerald Abraham 1974)

Modest Mussorgsky: his Life and Works, rev. Gerald Abraham (London, 1956)

Dahlhaus, Carl. *Realism in Nineteenth-Century Music*, trans. Mary Whittall (Cambridge, 1985)

Davies, Lawrence. *Ravel Orchestral Music* (London, 1970)

Edie, James M., Scanlan, James P. and Zeldin, Mary-Barbara. *Russian Philosophy* (Chicago, 1965), Vol. 2

Forte, Allen. 'Musorgsky as modernist', *Music Analysis*, 9 (1990), pp. 3–46

Frankenstein, Alfred. 'Victor Hartman and Modeste Musorgsky', *Musical Quarterly*, 25 (1939), pp. 268–91

Fried, Emilia. Notes accompanying Musorgsky, M. P. *Kartinki s vystavski*, facsimile autograph (Moscow, 1975)

Garden, Edward. *Balakirev* (London, 1967)

Hopkins, James F. 'Ravel's Orchestral Transcription Technique' (diss., Princeton U., 1969)

Hübsch, Lini. *Modest Mussorgskij 'Bilder einer Ausstellung'* (Munich, 1978)

Klein, Jason. 'Musorgsky's Pictures at an Exhibition: a Comparative Analysis of Several Orchestrations' (diss., Stanford U., 1980)

Kolodin, Irving. 'Everybody's Pictures', *Stereo Review* (March 1975), pp. 124–5

Leyda, Jay and Bertensson, Sergei. *The Musorgsky Reader* (New York, 1947); reprint (New York, 1970)

Montagu-Nathan, M. 'Hartmann and the Pictures from an Exhibition', *Monthly Musical Record*, 46 (1916), pp. 191–3

'New light on Moussorgsky's Pictures', *Monthly Musical Record*, 47 (1917), pp. 105–6

Newmarch, Rosa. *The Concert-Goer's Library of Descriptive Notes* (London, 1930), Vol. 3

Olkhovsky, Yuri. *Vladimir Stasov and Russian National Culture* (Ann Arbor, 1983)

Orlova, Alexandra. *Musorgsky's Days and Works: a Biography in Documents*, trans. Roy Guenther (Ann Arbor, 1983)

Puffett, Derrick. 'A graphic analysis of Musorgsky's "Catacombs"', *Music Analysis*, 9 (1990), pp. 67–78

Reilly, Edward R. *The Music of Mussorgsky: a Guide to the Editions* (New York, 1980)

Ridenour, Robert C. *Nationalism, Modernism and Personal Rivalry in Nineteenth-Century Russian Music* (Ann Arbor, 1981)

Rimsky-Korsakov, Nikolay. *My Musical Life*, trans. Judah A. Joffe (New York, 1942); revised edition (London, 1974)

Schnitke, A. 'Pictures from an Exhibition by M. P. Musorgsky', *Voprosy Muzykoznaniya*, 1 (1953–4), pp. 327–9 [in Russian only]

Seaman, Gerald R. *History of Russian Music* (Oxford, 1967), Vol. 1

Serov, Victor. *Modest Musorgsky* (New York, 1968)

Stasov, Vladimir. 'Selected Articles on Musorgsky', trans. Richard Hoops (diss., Florida State U., 1977)

Swan, Alfred J. 'The nature of Russian folk-song', *Musical Quarterly*, 29 (1949), pp. 498–516

Swan, Alfred J. *Russian Music and its Sources in Chant and Folk-Song* (London, 1973)

Taruskin, Richard. 'Realism as preached and practiced: the Russian opera dialogue', *Musical Quarterly*, 56 (1970), pp. 431–54

'Chernomor to Kashchei: harmonic sorcery; or Stravinsky's angle', *Journal of the American Musicological Society*, 38 (1985), pp. 72–142

Turner, June. 'Musorgsky', *Music Review*, 47 (1986–7), pp. 153–75

Valkenier, Elizabeth. *Russian Realist Art* (Ann Arbor, 1977)

Walker, James. 'Musorgsky's *Sunless* cycle in Russian criticism: focus of controversy', *Musical Quarterly*, 3 (1981), pp. 382–91

Index

Printed in the United Kingdom
by Lightning Source UK Ltd.
123384UK00001BA/2/A